One minute a toddler can be an angel, next moment a bawling, kicking, unreasoning tyrant. A source of great joy, and of frustration or despair.

This book is designed to help parents when they often need help and advice most. Brenda Crowe, author of *The Playgroup Movement* and National Adviser to the Pre-school Playgroups Association, explains what it is like to be a toddler and what it feels like to look after one. Many parents have had little contact with children before their first child is born. They are utterly unprepared for the impact on their lives of a small creature who suddenly begins to walk, run and climb – and to investigate everything and everywhere with no sense of danger.

Brenda Crowe gives a marvellously vivid picture of a toddler's world. She also offers a wealth of advice about a hundred and one aspects of living together – washing and dressing, meals, bedtime, outings, talking and listening, sharing the housework, helping each other – and how to deal with balking, tantrums and sleeping and eating problems. She also gives a fascinating and revealing account of her own and other parents' experience of parenthood and discusses how to cope with the tiredness, loneliness and depression which can wear down even the most capable and cheerful parent.

GW00671630

By the same author

THE PLAYGROUP MOVEMENT
PLAYGROUP ACTIVITIES

With Kenneth Jameson

WHAT'S A HOUSE?

Living with a Toddler

BRENDA CROWE

Foreword by Willem van der Eyken

London
UNWIN PAPERBACKS
Boston   Sydney

First published in Great Britain by George Allen & Unwin 1980
First published in Unwin Paperbacks 1982
Reprinted 1983
This book is copyright under the Berne Convention. No reproduction
without permission. All rights reserved.

UNWIN® PAPERBACKS
40 Museum Street, London, WC1A 1LU, UK

Unwin Paperbacks
Park Lane, Hemel Hempstead, Herts HP2 4TE, UK

George Allen & Unwin Australia Pty Ltd,
8 Napier Street, North Sydney, NSW 2060, Australia

© Brenda Crowe, 1980, 1982
Foreword © Willem van der Eyken, 1980

British Library Cataloguing in Publication Data

Crowe, Brenda
  Living with a toddler.—(Unwin paperbacks)
1. Parent and child   2. Children—
Management
I. Title
306.8′7   HQ769
ISBN 0-04-649015-9

Set in 12 on 13 point Baskerville by Typesetters (Birmingham) Ltd,
and printed in Great Britain
by Hazell Watson & Viney Ltd, Aylesbury, Bucks.

Foreword

As Brenda Crowe so lucidly points out in this book, 'the birth of a baby is also the simultaneous birth of two parents'. But, unlike the new baby, our own birth is a case of having to be born again, a painful and often frustrating process that does not always lead to happy fulfilment. We discover this most forcefully when baby turns toddler, for parenting a toddler, as this book graphically illustrates, takes uncommon resources, endless patience and a boundless sense of humour, just when we discover that we do not possess unlimited supplies of any of these commodities. The result is often anger, frustration and inevitably a painful reassessment of ourselves as people; for what children always ask of us, constantly and loudly, is: 'Who are you?'

Being a parent demands a perpetual metamorphosis as one's comfortable dogmas, assumptions, taboos and foibles are challenged, overthrown, mocked or denied. Moreover, this readjustment takes place within two differing time scales: clock-time against development-time. 'The golden rule is – not to hurry children,' says Brenda Crowe, while recognising in saying it that the bus will not wait, the shops will soon close, the washing cries out to be done, that our clockwork world makes incessant demands on our time and patience. Here lie the seeds of conflict, and ultimately – if we are lucky, and have generous children – of our own self-education and growth. For in wrestling with our priorities, in resolving these opposing tensions, we, too, gradually shape for ourselves a self-identity that can become a source of strength and comfort.

In this process, we cannot wish for a better guide than Brenda Crowe. For ten years she was National Adviser to the Pre-school Playgroups Association, as it grew from a small pioneering band to become one of the most impressive populist movements in the country. As the parents who speak through her pages testify, she has lent her attentive ear and cast her sympathetic eye over thousands of parent–child relationships, developing her deep knowledge and passing it on to many of us who have listened to, and learnt from, her. But I prefer the image she lightly sketches of herself here: sitting contentedly sewing within the confines of a homely play-pen, while her own children play outside, unable to get at the pins, needles and thread that might endanger them. This domestic example of lateral thinking, of improvisation, of a happy accommodation between adult demands and child needs, represents what the playgroups movement really means. It has never been content to be merely a voluntary response to a national need for more day care; rather, it is a positive affirmation of children, parenting and family life.

These pages reflect that view. Brenda Crowe's philosophy is suffused with her innate respect for the child. It recalls Geoffrey Pyke, the founder of the Malting House School in the twenties, when he remarked that 'the fundamental principle we should follow in dealing with children is to treat every child as a distinguished foreign visitor who knows little or nothing of our language or customs'. Just so Brenda Crowe invites us to shrink our world down to two-foot nothing, and to observe it populated by bawling, tugging giants – a thoughtless, often a cruel and frightening place. She draws us into this realm through her natural empathy with our hesitations, uncertainties and bewilderment when faced with the urgent, persistent demands of our toddler.

'Don't be intimidated by what other people think,' she urges – but, alas, most of us *are* the prisoners of our preconceived reflections of other people. And therein lies the joy of children – they are free of such imposed constraints. Knowing nothing of conformity, fashion or taboo, they can make us children again too, and enable us to see our own world afresh.

This book should be enjoyed like a slow mint. Armed only with a toddler and the following pages, it would be a pity to hurry the creative, shared experiences that Brenda Crowe offers, or the cumulative effects they could have on any mother's or father's relationship with their young child.

Willem van der Eyken
London, 1979

Acknowledgements

Particular thanks are due to Vera Hughes for all her typing and patient help; to Doris Mobbs for encouraging so many parents to bridge the gap between meaning to write and writing and to the parents who wrote so naturally and honestly.

Contents

Part 1
Parents' and Toddlers' Feelings

How my Viewpoint Changed

This isn't a book about babies, it is a book about toddlers and it is written in the hope that it may boost a parent's confidence just at the moment when it sometimes takes a hard knock.

Childbirth affects every woman differently and the individual variations in health, happiness and confidence of mothers, together with the relationship of new parents to each other and their baby, deserve a book to themselves: but this isn't it. This book is for those parents who find themselves unprepared for the impact on their lives of a small child who begins to sleep less during the day; to walk, run and climb, to investigate anything and everything with no sense of danger; and, more and more frequently, to change with bewildering suddenness from a loving, responsive and amenable angel into an unco-operative and defiant little monster – and back again.

If this is the phase through which your child is passing at the moment, take heart, stop asking yourself where you went wrong, and accept that your child is paying you a compliment. It is precisely because you have brought up a normal, happy, healthy, confident, curious child that this new stage of development is upon you.

This is the stage when children experiment with physical and emotional independence; and no matter how many children you have, the difference in their individual temperaments, noticeable perhaps even from birth, will become markedly clearer as the opportunities for experiment widen and their personalities develop. And it is at this stage that you will probably discover that something of a gap exists between what books and experts tell you to expect and do and your own physical, emotional and imaginative ability to cope with your toddler's demands and behaviour.

Many years ago I trained as a nursery school teacher, and well remember how we walked out of our hostel having eaten the breakfast put before us, sat in lecture rooms that someone else had cleaned and heated, enjoyed lively discussions with intelligent, well informed lecturers who gave us their undivided attention, and trooped back into the dining room to eat a lunch that had been bought, cooked and served for us.

We worked conscientiously for hours every night, but nobody interrupted us with rival claims on our time and attention. We carefully prepared ourselves before spending a morning with the children, and nothing and no one came between us and them. We went back to the hostel for another prepared meal, and returned to the lecture room to study the work of the great educators. At the end of three years we knew a great deal about the theory of education, and were told that as the years went by our experience would make the theory come alive. Although this was true for many, I can only say that it just didn't happen for me.

I was nervous and excited about my first job, but eventually settled into a happy and confident routine. The children blossomed and the parents seemed grateful for the advice I offered so freely. I recalled a great deal that I had learned by watching our college lecturers working with under-fives, and linked that experience with my own as I watched, listened and learned.

I learned a great deal from the children, but sadly I learned much less from their parents. It may have been that I was too busy trying to teach them, but it may also have been that I wasn't emotionally geared to learning about the realities of parenthood at that stage, as I was caught up in the excitement of being engaged and I romantically assumed that one day we would be the splendid parents of splendid children.

In fact, I had always thought that I was a rather good nursery school teacher, and confidently expected to be an

4

even better mother. When the time came I was totally unprepared for the vast difference between looking after other people's children and looking after our own. When our own children arrived, I at last understood how mothers felt when they saw the children at the top of the climbing frame, while the teacher blandly assured them that they were perfectly safe. At last I understood their irrational fear that their children might get wet feet playing with water and that damp socks might lead to a chill, pneumonia and death. At last I knew how mothers felt when a morning's ironing was pulled on to the floor, the sugar was tipped into the milk jug, a small bedroom slipper was flushed down the lavatory and the cat was fed with the fish intended for us.

Coping with children and chores for an unbroken twelve-hour day is a mammoth undertaking and, even if our college staff hoped that our theory would come alive in our nursery school practice, it was less realistic to assume that it would also come alive in the very different context of our own homes. It certainly didn't for me. I was too busy, too tired, and too involved with the children to be free to observe, recall, think, interpret and relate theory to practice.

I also viewed our own children in terms of a totally different time scale. Each family has its own sense of history, and parents look back as well as forward. Is this or that characteristic inherited? Is this Uncle Joe coming out? If so, can things be different this time round? It is easy enough to tell other parents not to worry or that their children will grow out of such and such a phase, but it is not so easy to reassure yourself as these same phases surprisingly hit you and yours. Conversely, does a chance masterpiece or a bandaged doll mean that there is another budding artist or doctor in the family? It is sometimes difficult to see each child as he really is when the physical, emotional and historical ties of the family are so close.

The one thing that helped me enormously was my

good fortune in having worked with so many, different toddlers before I had to combine my own first taste of motherhood with the job of wife, cook, cleaner, economist, nurse, dressmaker, gardener and decorator. Many women come to motherhood, which is one of the most important, responsible, demanding and creative jobs of a lifetime, with virtually no experience of young children at all. And on top of that some are single parents and others have no choice but to work full-time.

It is at this crucial point that confidence can take a hard knock. We assume that because we are mature and intelligent adults we are not at the mercy of our emotions and that we can confidently turn to friends or books for reassurance or advice. So it is demoralising to discover that one small child can repeatedly reduce us to the verge of tears and that not only do friends and child-experts alike offer conflicting advice but their well-intended explanations and suggestions can reinforce the sense of failure we feel if we are too tired and defeated to muster the necessary patience, skill and sensitivity as we try to maintain a balance between the needs of a very demanding toddler and the never-ending chain of household chores.

In fact, few parents are prepared for the unmentionable truth that a toddler can and often does make a sane and normally self-possessed adult behave exactly like a toddler. Far from being an admission of failure it can be positively valuable to catch yourself out in this way, for the very fact that you have the honesty to recognise the truth is a step in the right direction. At any age what we are is more important than what we know. In these first few years of parenthood it is possible to redress the mental habits of a lifetime and learn not to overvalue knowledge and to undervalue the personal qualities that turn knowledge into wisdom.

I listened to worn-out parents throughout my wartime nursery school days, and to distressed parents during my

years at a child guidance clinic, and to eager, thought-
ful playgroup parents when I first met them as we tried
together to shape a local course that would help them at
home as well as in their playgroups, but above all I have
listened to parents all over the country during ten years
as National Adviser to the Pre-school Playgroups
Association.

The playgroup movement reaffirmed for me that the
apparently deep divisions in society of wealth, housing,
jobs, politics, religion, education and culture are in reality
only superficial, and that at the deepest levels of human
experience there is unity. Birth and the early years of
parenthood are such an experience, and there isn't a
single hope, fear, doubt, frustration, pride, joy, anger,
bewilderment, pleasure, tragedy, thankfulness, satisfaction, despair or state of mind, body or soul that I haven't
encountered constantly in every kind of community in the
country – and few that I haven't experienced myself.

Although the emotions and their causes are so common
to us all, parents experience them to a different degree,
encounter them at different stages, and express them in
different ways. Therefore I wanted mothers and fathers to
speak through the following pages in their own words in
the hope that as many other parents as possible may be
able to say 'That's me!' from time to time as they read.

As so often happens I didn't have to sit down and
'decide' how to go about this, it 'happened' and I went
along with it because it felt natural and comfortably right.
I was invited once again to speak in an area with which
I have come to feel deeply involved over the years, and
as I drove the sixty miles the conviction grew that this
was the community to which I would turn for help.

It is a small country town with ever-growing council
and private housing estates in the London commuter
belt, built on the very steep sides of a valley with a main
road dividing the hillside communities still further. A
new town lies to one side of it, and a relatively undisturbed

little town on the other. A Branch of the Pre-school Playgroups Association is the meeting-point for those involved in the Mother and Toddler Clubs, playgroups, informal courses, back-up systems and social life that are so intertwined that no one quite knows whether they are working or playing.

Ten years ago I first visited a single playgroup lovingly run on a stage at the end of a small hall. Slowly grandparents and teenagers were drawn in and even more slowly home 'meetings to talk about things' evolved into courses that now meet different needs in different ways and places (one of which is home meetings again for the new generation of mothers). 'Talks' to the teenagers in school led to a mother and toddler club being started there, in which both the girls and boys began to understand how endearing, challenging and exhausting these younger children can be. A newsletter appeared, and 'news' was soon being augmented by enthusiastic, nostalgic and sometimes painful contributions from three generations of women and men sharing their experiences for the benefit of others. I have talked with this ever-widening group of parents at intervals over the years, and phone calls and letters have kept me in touch with each new development, excitement and despair, build-up and let-down, stalemate and progress.

During the last year the parents have known that I was trying to write a book that would be as much for them as about their children, and I asked for their help in telling me what they thought parenthood would be like, and what it actually was like when it came.

The letters and jottings began to trickle in – long ones, short ones, beautifully tabulated ones and spontaneous outpourings, on notepaper, file paper, toddler club painting paper, sheets torn from jotting pads and exercise books, and even one on a paper hand towel. Some husbands and wives wrote independently, then compared notes and sent both letters just as they were; others wrote independently but the wives confessed that they had destroyed their husbands' letters. But there were some parents whose thoughts and feelings were very important although they were unlikely to reach me by letter, and here the gap was bridged by my long-time link, now a granny but still at the heart of all that is happening.

She has a gift for listening, almost total recall, and a capacious handbag in which she just 'happens to have' scrap paper and biros for those who need them on the spur of the moment. During her usual chats and listening she asked mothers and fathers what they imagined it would be like to have a baby, and what they felt like now that their children were toddlers. She found that every single parent was articulate, some poured it out, some thought silently before answering, some let it come in fits and starts, and when they had finished she told them about the book and said how much it would help other parents if they could jot down some of the things that they had just said, adding 'I've got some odds and ends of paper if you'd like to.'

Many were prepared to 'jot' then and there, while it was fresh in their minds and with Granny to act as a carrier pigeon between them and me. Others said they couldn't write it down, 'but you can tell 'er if you like'. No one has been quoted and nothing has been reproduced without permission, and where a quotation appears out of context it exists alone in the spirit in which it was intended. There has been no attempt at 'research' or 'random sampling' or anything like that because this isn't that sort of book. What follows is simply the written and spoken experiences of parents in a particular community that will reach out to many of you in widely different communities.

If their experiences reflect your own and parenthood came as something of a shock, then I hope you will be reassured to discover that you are not alone. And if you can identify some of your own expectations of being a

9

parent and compare them with present realities then you may be able to trace some difficulties back to false expectations, both of yourself and your toddler.

This book is an attempt to present both a toddler's view of being a toddler and a parent's view of being a parent, in the hope that you may discover how many feelings and needs you have in common. As you acknowledge each other's feelings and try to meet each other's needs you will create a relationship in which you can grow and develop as much as your toddler. These years at home are not 'wasted', they can be the prelude to a fuller life than you have yet known – once you have adjusted to the tiredness and responsibility of these first years.

One last point that needs to be made in this sex-role-conscious age – in using 'you' I am assuming that the reader is just as likely to be a father as a mother and it shouldn't be assumed that fathers are only referred to when they are mentioned specifically. I know from experience that it is just as likely that it is the father who goes to a crying child in the night as the mother. The 'you' may also be a grandparent, childminder, nurse, student or anyone else who lives, works or stays with toddlers from time to time. Similarly 'he' may well be a 'she', but it seems less clumsy than 'he or she' each time – our own first-born happened to be a 'he' and, as it is particularly the parents of first-borns that I have in mind, that was the pronoun that came most naturally.

How it Feels to be a Parent

'What you ought to be told at ante-natal clinics is 'ow yer can commit murder without being caught. If that was possible my two would've had it by now – *wouldn't* yer? – but yer lovely little buggers!'

So said a mother, putting it in a nutshell for many. The words of other parents which follow express the feelings and experience of many more.

'Perhaps I am oversensitive, but I am very affected by what I feel other people expect me to do – like get cross and smack him when I don't think I should, or the other way round.'

'It was going to be lovely – that's just the general impression that I had. But now after two years I'm so exhausted. My doctor says Paul has an overactive brain – I call it just not sleeping!'

'My husband and I didn't used to have rows and arguments before the children. He thinks I'm too soft – he expects them to be grown up *now*, and often I go for them just to keep him quiet.'

'I didn't think it would be all plain sailing with a toddler, but I thought I could discipline him and control him when it was needed. I didn't reckon with an extremely independent and headstrong child. The battle of wits is sometimes won by him, sometimes by me. The conclusion I've reached is that one has to be very adaptable and not to feel a failure as a mother when things don't work out as you think they should.'

11

'I tend to be a realist or even a cynic and before my first pregnancy was a great believer that being a housewife would hold little satisfaction. As it turns out I believe that this is the most satisfying period of my life so far.'

'Having a baby means that I have given up any right to my own thoughts or pleasures, certainly during the day . . . How does one amuse children all day long? I always feel guilty if James seems to be bored. There's a lot of feeling guilty about motherhood.'

'I didn't think playing with a 15-month-old baby would be so much fun. Having a baby has its good times and bad times but I think the good times are far greater than the bad times and I wouldn't have missed the experience of being a parent for anything.'

'Being the mother of a toddler is basically as I anticipated, but being the mother of an asthmatic toddler is something that is taking me quite a while to get used to.'

'No one prepared me for the awful feeling of responsibility that descended within days of giving birth, feelings of inadequacy especially after having a career, feeling that I had become a completely different person and can now never revert to the "me" that was before. Therefore my whole life has changed irrevocably – but not, I hasten to add, for the worse.'

These comments and extracts from letters represent a wide cross-section of discoveries common to parents everywhere, and those of you who may have felt isolated in your experience will probably feel relieved to discover that you are not alone.

Grouping together some of the following reflections may make it clearer that we are the bridges between our own parents and our children. It is true that 'the sins of the fathers (and mothers) are visited upon the children unto the third and fourth generation', but it is also true that good mothering and fathering is handed down the generations too. Our past doesn't have to be our children's future, especially if we can learn from each other and build on all that is positive.

Although this is a book about toddlers it is very relevant to take into consideration how both parents felt before, during and after the birth, for these early feelings and experiences can sometimes affect the relationship between parents and their children for quite a long time.

The following letters may also be helpful for those hoping to have more children, for no two pregnancies or babies are alike and other people's experience may be yours next time.

Anticipation

'About the only mental picture of what it [having children] would be like that I can remember is visualising a warm sunny day, walking in the woods, with the children running happily from twig to twig, examining everything, excitedly calling out discoveries . . . The reality of this picture is far from true. My older boy (3½ nearly) is ghastly out walking – he just wants to be carried, and although he has now given up that request he drags along slowly, twiddling his hair (his answer to thumb sucking). He does occasionally revive for things like hide and seek, or if we do something really out of the ordinary – but it is a real effort to keep him happy on a walk.'

'[I imagined] a cosy routine of feeding, playing and sleeping in the first few weeks, and plenty of visitors. I remember thinking that mother nature had played a particularly dirty trick by making me more exhausted than I had ever been at a time when I needed the most energy!'

' "Yes, Mrs — the test is positive. Goodbye." No congratulations or how pleased you must be, just the cold clinical term "positive". Now what do you do, wait for the father-to-be to return from work or do you ring? No, wait until he returns to see his reaction. And then you think, what about my reaction? How do I feel, should it be the greatest moment in my life being told that I am to endure another six or seven months of discomfort waiting for a baby that I haven't the faintest idea what I will do with when or if it arrives safely? I do remember feeling very excited at the thought of telling my family and friends. I think there is something very special about a first pregnancy and a first grandchild. However, I had a great cloud in my mind that I might be one of the unlucky mothers who produce a handicapped or mentally subnormal baby . . . .'

'Having worked with computers doing programming for ten years, I had a tendency to expect the baby to behave predictably as if programmed. I expected all problems of sleeping, feeding, crying, etc., to have identifiable causes and therefore straightforward solutions. The ante-natal classes had not indicated how much guesswork was involved in caring for the needs of a new baby and that many "problems" may just be normal behaviour for that child. I had imagined that babies and children were given toys and books, etc., with which they amused themselves. The reality of a child who from the age of four months expected to be entertained in all his waking hours was a big shock.'

We all have our expectations about all sorts of things, founded on observation, linked memories, reading, advertising, romantic or anxious imagination, or our own hidden needs. No one can tell parents-to-be what they will think and feel during pregnancy but the wide range of emotions and imaginings could at least be indicated during the period of ante-natal care. False expectations are the cause of much of our shock and disappointment at every stage and age, but this is particularly true of parenthood.

Schools are increasingly involved with 'preparation for parenthood' courses for both boys and girls, but since you can't adequately prepare anyone for anything as yet outside their experience it becomes increasingly clear that one of the best forms of preparation for the future is consolidation of the past. This means helping young people to make good missed play experiences, offering them opportunities to be with babies and playing children, and helping them to understand their relationships with their own parents.

The link between schools, mother and toddler clubs and playgroups is a happy and valuable one, providing as it does for young people to be with the whole age range from birth to five years, to talk to parents, to share the children's play, and to see how the parents in charge of the children create a happy atmosphere by balancing freedom and control. In the discussion that follows these visits it is particularly important that parents are not 'blamed', for all too soon these young people will have children of their own and will discover how their parents felt, and why they did and said what they did once their babies arrived and were their responsibility day after day after day: they will need to feel that society supports rather than blames them.

The Impact of Pregnancy and Birth on Fathers

'I can remember very clearly the feeling that came over me when my wife walked up the garden path after coming back from phoning the doctor to get confirmation [of pregnancy]. She didn't have to tell me, I could tell from her face. She had a smile literally from ear to ear.

15

I think it must have been a contagious smile because I could feel myself smiling in the same manner. I felt extremely happy but in a very strange sort of way. This was something I had never thought about, it was a new kind of happiness, something I knew nothing about. A kind of frightened happiness.

'The following morning I awoke feeling very excited and decided that I just couldn't cope with going to work. So I phoned in to work and told my boss that I was unable to attend work because I was pregnant. After a few seconds of silence he congratulated me and told me he would pass the good news on to my workmates.

'Now came the time to tell our parents the news. Now, this was a strange experience, in fact very difficult to put into words. We knew that everybody would be delighted, but to actually tell one's own parents seemed very difficult, almost as though we had done something wrong and had to confess to it. A sort of embarrassment really but as soon as the news was broken the reaction from both sets of parents completely changed that feeling into one of great pride.

'I had agreed to be present at birth but I wasn't really certain if I was brave enough. This uncertainty soon changed the morning I was awoken and told not to get ready for work. From then on nothing was going to keep me from seeing my child born. So for the next 31 hours I ate and drank very little and didn't sleep, but I didn't feel hungry, thirsty or tired.

'When Daniel was born I was completely numb. I found it very difficult to associate the newly born baby, that I could see, with the "thing" that had been kicking my hand for the past few months. I was very choked when the nurse handed baby Daniel to me to hold.'

'The one thing I was never able to comprehend was that there was a baby growing in the womb and in the later months it was moving, living in there, and when it was

16

born the first thing it would do is breathe. Of course we knew we would have a baby but when I was told we had a girl I was on cloud nine. When I saw her I was just lost for words – another stage of my life, a feeling of fulfilment. When I went home that night having spent from 8 a.m. to 9 p.m. at the hospital I was drained but to realise that back at the hospital was our girl gave a strange feeling of elation.'

'Then the baby arrives – horrible, ugly, bloody, purple. But look again. It's the most perfectly beautiful little girl in the whole world. It's the most emotional moment I've ever experienced. [Of the second birth] Then again the magic moment arrives . . . It's all over. Another baby daughter arrives, looks the same as last time. Despite it being the second time around the emotion, feelings, etc., are still the same. No way are they diminished – that perfect moment of arrival and the first cry, the tears of relief, love and all the other feelings that are released by the breaking of the tension of the birth. [Of the third birth] Guess what? It's a boy. I can't explain it, back came all the feelings, emotion, tears just as though it was the first time all over again. I should think, that if we were to have twelve children it would always be the same.'

'The first time I saw her I cannot tell you the feeling – wonderful, wonderful. I shall never forget. And I felt also a great responsibility. This must be universal.'

'Post-natal depression – you read about this; however, it has to be experienced to be understood. I did not realise that your wife becomes depressed so, and it is a time for tact, etc., and with attention they grow out of it, not immediately though.'

17

The Impact of Pregnancy and Birth on Mothers

'My colleagues [all said], "How marvellous, you must be delighted." "Oh yes, of course," I said, but felt nothing. My indifference continued for the following nine months, although I was quite well and continued working, and although I had always wanted a baby, I did not bother to make many garments or get the nursery ready. I was not really interested . . . When Hugh Anthony was born I was relieved that it was all over, but I did not really take a great interest in him until he came home from hospital. As time passed I grew more and more fond of him . . . my indifference before he was born certainly turned to love and enthusiasm and I am glad I am not working so that I can look after him full-time.'

'I couldn't really associate my lump with a baby, even at the late stage when ten days overdue and still waiting I felt I was just going to be relieved of an unpleasant illness rather than actually help the doctor and nurses with the delivery of my baby. And yet I attended the relaxation classes and saw films about feeding baby, bathing baby, and my husband and I had prepared for its arrival with all the necessities . . . but somehow I felt strangely detached from it all.

'But when B-day did finally arrive and I was presented with a perfectly formed little baby girl my husband and I both felt we had created a miracle.'

'. . . so came the great day when Emma was born. After spending ten hours in hospital in heavy labour, a Caesarean was needed. The specialist was called out and an hour later Emma was placed in my husband's arms.

'She was brought to me three days later to be fed (may I say that this was at about 9.30ish at night). I thought,

18

"Oh my God what is this screaming mass – surely not mine!" After repeated attempts at trying to feed her they decided on a bottle. The same happened in the morning, so we decided on the bottle. To be honest, I didn't want to feed her, that mother feeling they say happens when you see your baby didn't happen.

'When I left hospital twelve days later that feeling still hadn't happened (in fact it took a good three months). When I arrived home I was terrified. I sat in a chair every day for six weeks waiting for the next feed and had heart failure if she woke half an hour or so before a feed. That improved, I am glad to say. Then came the next stage – feeding solids to a baby who was desperate for food and who didn't like solids. I sat howling and so did she. After three weeks of this I did what most health visitors say not to do – give some milk first, then the food. This worked and after a short time she did eat.

'My real motherly instincts came when she was about ten months old.'

'It is almost impossible to remember exactly what one thought before – everything is very hazy as if the person one was *before* one became a mother has just dissolved into thin air. I thought I would be totally indifferent to the baby, feeling neither positive love nor dislike, but only nothingness, though I never doubted that I would look after "it" perfectly well physically, as if it were a dog or guinea-pig I had been asked to care for. Babies had never aroused my interest in the way that cats or hamsters, for example, do, and I couldn't see that my own [baby] would be any different. In fact I was rather worried about this lack of mother love.

'When I first saw her (I was heavily sedated from Caesarean Section) I instantly felt very protective, thinking "poor little thing" and "she doesn't look like me – I can't believe she's part of me", and I reached out to touch her head. After feeling relatively normal and free of saline drips, etc., I thoroughly enjoyed cuddling her and "patting" her in her cot, and for several weeks felt indifferent to my cats.'

'I thought I had prepared myself mentally for motherhood. What I had not expected were the enormous physical and emotional demands that confronted me. I have never experienced such extremes of emotion as I did in the first four–five months of Andrew's life: great joy, utter exhaustion, intense anxiety, enormous pleasure. All came tumbling one on top of the other. I remember losing a lot of self-confidence at first. I had thoroughly enjoyed teaching and I was used to managing thirty children. Now, here I was finding it very difficult to meet the demands of only one little boy . . . I had not allowed for the fact that a baby could take over so completely and I was surprised to find my own personality totally submerged in those first months. I found also that I became very sensitive to observations about Andrew made by others. I tended to take harmless comments about routine, etc., as personal criticism.

'I can see now how much of my emotional state was as a direct result of my health. Pregnancy and birth are draining and the body needs time to adjust and return to normal.'

Birth may be a perfectly natural event, but those who have been through it too easily forget that every mother goes through the age-old process from conception to delivery and after-birth as though she was the first to whom it had ever happened. No amount of 'preparation' can ever prepare a woman or a man for their *feelings* at the birth of their child (whether it be elation, rejection or something between the two), and it is their *feelings* that they take home with them together with their baby. And yet many women emerge from this overwhelming experience feeling that they have been part of a production-line process through the clinic, labour ward, recovery ward and home again without ever having time to savour the climax of nine months' build-up – still less to recognise that the birth of the baby was also the simultaneous birth of two parents.

Still more worrying is the number of mothers who for one of many reasons are 'robbed' of their newborn babies for days, only to feel indifference or dangerous hostility when the baby is suddenly given back to them and they are left alone together.

As a farmer's daughter I can still remember the night-long bawling of the cows whose calves had been taken from them at birth, just as vividly as I can recall sows, ewes and chickens rejecting or killing their offspring if they were over-handled or removed temporarily for resuscitation: the separation of mother and offspring is against nature, and increasingly this is being recognised by doctors and midwives. If a baby has to be removed from the mother, for example to be put into intensive care, and if it is truly impossible for her to be taken to see and touch her baby, then it is imperative that someone finds the time to explain exactly what is happening, to share her feeling of total loss, and to be there to reintroduce mother and child to each other when the reunion finally takes place. This is a sensitive period and the mother may need help and reassurance.

The Influence of Parents' Parents

'When we were expecting a child, we spent a long time thinking over what things we would do with him, how we would bring him up.

'We were both agreed that we wanted to bring up our child neither in an authoritarian manner, as we both had very strict parents, nor did we want to bring him up too permissively as it is important to recognise natural authority . . .

21

'Although the child is an individual personality many things have to be forcibly inculcated by the parents (influence of the environment). When does this educative process begin, and how? By discipline, by talking to the child, by punishment, etc.? What we lack most here is the example of our parents. For in many situations one reacts according to what one has experienced oneself as a child at home, although one is always telling oneself that this mode of upbringing is not ours.'

'I find myself time and time again shouting out the same threatening phrases my mother used to shout at us when her patience had run out and often have to laugh at myself. Indeed, I find myself mimicking her tone of voice.'

'I keep seeing glimpses of my brother's temperament in my daughter, this gives rise to mixed feelings; one thing is certain we shall have our hands full in years to come' (from a father).

'I am pleased when I look back to my childhood; the things that used to worry and upset me as a child, I now make sure that these things don't worry my child, i.e. I remember what it is like to be afraid of the unknown and parents not having time to listen to me. So I try all the harder to listen and understand my children's problems' (from a father).

No one mentioned the unexpected snags in looking back to an ideal childhood with 'perfect' parents. Many young parents idealise their own parents and strive to live up to their standard – never shouting, never smacking, never being impatient, always being reasonable, understanding and loving – and then feel guilty at their failure, or nervously exhausted, because with all this giving out to their children they are denying some of their own basic needs. If you fall into this category remember that distance lends enchantment: it is very unlikely that your parents really were this perfect, but because the overall memory of your childhood is one of goodness and happiness you have forgotten about the atmospheres of silent disapproval, the periods of nervous prostration, the hurt feelings and the overprotectiveness that are so often part of being a 'perfect parent' – not to mention the suppression of aggressive feelings to such a degree that children find themselves totally unprepared to face the hurly-burly of the neighbourhood and playground.

Remember, too, that love may even now blind you to the fact that you have adopted your parents' attitudes to everything without question instead of rethinking every habit, attitude and belief for yourself in the light of your own circumstances, relationships and the times in which you live. This is not disloyalty, this is the ultimate compliment that children pay their parents – the compliment of growing up to be themselves, not copies of anybody else, however dearly loved.

Because memories of being mothered and fathered are so strong, and may be less than adequate, there is a great need for parents to see other adults relating to children and this is one of the great strengths of the playgroup movement and mother and toddler clubs. Parents can see several different adults coping with a variety of situations in different ways, and they therefore have not just one but a choice of models on which to base their own experiments of copying and adapting.

Distressing Discoveries

'On a bad day, when I'm feeling frayed at the edges, then being a mother can be a thoroughly painful experience. There is almost a physical feeling of frustration, that I am trapped and would give anything for a couple of hours away from the fray. In other words I don't have as much patience as I had expected for in reality I am not really a trapped or isolated mother, as one knows many mothers are.'

'On looking back I think the greatest loss to a mother-to-be is her freedom to be an individual. I feel a woman gives up everything for her child whereas a man still continues his routine of work and hobbies, as I think it is commonly accepted, a sort of unwritten law, that it is the woman's job to look after her child, especially during the first five years, and then I think the father plays a more important role in the family.'

'[Life is] very difficult without transport. Carrying nappies, food, baby in papoose and bags of shopping is no joke. Not so much better now. For example, last week I had to take my toddler plus pushchair and haversack by public transport and escalators (no lifts available) to Newcastle. I had to ask people to help me. Feelings of anger and frustration when having to shop. For instance Mothercare accessible only by escalator or three flights of steps! The intolerant attitude of most bus drivers – men! – and idiot planners who never think.'

'I think tiredness is my worst enemy . . .
    'How difficult it is to keep control of yourself. The number of times I have actually felt like shaking the living daylights out of them. I don't think one realises how upsetting and trying motherhood can be – not until it has been experienced. My little girl went through a phase of shouting and being very rude to people, especially relatives. I know I shout at them both sometimes, which isn't like me at all. My husband doesn't like it, I don't like it but I just don't seem able to stop myself sometimes! So then I have a feeling of guilt when she behaves like this – in fact blaming myself completely . . . People don't believe me when I tell them, because they say I am so placid with the children. So then I feel even worse – I

feel as though I'm putting on an act! Possibly it is a feeling of being cut off and closed in – I used to teach in a secondary school. I must admit I often feel very jealous when my husband talks about his involvement with school. Yet the silly thing is, I have no urgent desire to get back to work for a few years at least, so why these feelings!'

'. . . he started playing up in the night, more so as I put him to bed. This made me tired and irritable; this caused a lot of friction between me and my husband especially when I had been up two and three times a night . . . I didn't realise that bringing up a child would be so difficult, when to say "No" and when a smack is needed. I have never liked hitting children but I don't like children that are rude, or bad-mannered, so I set about to try and guide my child. There are so many different theories on discipline and bringing up children. I attended a lecture by Penelope Leach on "Parenthood, Partnership or Dictatorship?" which was very helpful. But it has to be agreed by mother and father which path to take.'

Several times parents commented on the fact that rows came after the children, which seems to suggest that not only do boys and girls need to think about their own relationship with their parents while they are still at school, but that time needs to be found during ante-natal preparation for parents to discuss what sort of relationship they hope to have with their own children, and how they hope to achieve their aims.

Many of the painful feelings experienced by mothers and fathers arise from their disappointment in themselves: they feel guilty, ashamed and angry that one small child has driven them to shout, smack, and even hit, when this isn't what they wanted or intended to do. Often their expectations of their children and themselves have been set too high, and no allowances have been made for the dire effects of disturbed nights and insufficient sleep, and the inevitable physical and nervous strain and drain of maintaining constant guard over toddlers who have energy, mobility and no sense of danger or cause and effect.

Another cause of distress is the realisation for both parents, but particularly the mother if she is the one at home all day, that the whole course of their lives has changed. Many parents feel trapped, cut off, even extinguished as persons in their own right. One mother expressed this as a 'feeling that I had become a completely different person and can never revert to the "me" that was before. Therefore my whole life has changed irrevocably'. This mother then went on to say '. . . but not I hasten to add for the worse'. Not all parents feel this sense of compensation, and it needs to be said again and again that the end of the 'me' that was doesn't have to be 'the end of me'; it can and should be the beginning of a newer and fuller 'me'. But it should also be explained that this new stage of self-development sometimes begins with what feels like an obstacle race, if not a fully-fledged commando course – and no wonder that for some it literally turns into a tragic assault course. Other stresses can be set up within the family by conflicting views on convention and morality, and frequently this leads to housing complications. One father's experience will be that of many others:

'When Margaret was expecting our baby, I was very happy. My happiness was a little bit dampened as Margaret wasn't very happy about the coming birth. We hadn't been together long and Margaret's parents predicted that we wouldn't last six months. Anyway, in a matter of days we were both looking forward to the birth. Shortly after the news of the coming baby I was told that we would have to leave our flat as the owner was selling. This didn't help as I now had the worry of providing a home for us. As we weren't at the time married the local council said they couldn't help us. This was a great worry to me not being able to provide for my family. I felt very inadequate and unhappy. Friends offered a home in the end and things started looking up. When Michael was born I was slightly bemused, almost in a state of shock. I was very pleased to see Margaret and I remember thinking Michael had big feet. Later on the joy of it all sank in and I went telling people and celebrating. When Michael arrived home the biggest shock of all was Michael crying every night for two months. When we moved to a place of our own the crying stopped. I am sure Michael could sense the tension which inevitably occurs when living with other people.'

Pleasing Discoveries

'One's relationship with one's child starts very one-sided – you share all their joys and hardships, but they cannot share yours. Perhaps a measure of successful parenthood is how equal you can make the sharing? It was certainly pleasing the other day to see Katie laughing just because we happened to be laughing' (this was Katie's father).

'I think every stage is the best and think it is best to make the most of your children and get the most enjoyment from them because they give so much happiness and joy in our lives.'

'Compensations of being at home with young children are: the freedom to arrange what you do, within fairly wide limits; the pleasures of new achievements; seeing their pleasure and excitement at the new things and at special events.'

'The addition of twins to the family caused a pause for thought (no time for a long one though!) I theorised less and probably did more. They convinced one of there being no necessity to go mad with keeping everywhere ultra-presentable, and to spend the time saved by just being with the children.'

'I enjoy being a mother.'

'I never really understood my toddlers until it was nearly too late. Then I realised that I could actually enjoy them and I certainly did. But how I wish I had found out sooner!'

'Yet we are convinced, although between Martin and us there are certainly more violent "struggles" than between us and our parents, that Martin will be better prepared for life. And we hope he will have nicer memories of a happy childhood. We are trying to bring Martin up liberally and at the same time to equip him to fit into society so he will have a happy future.

'Any upbringing is useless if the child does not feel wanted, if he is not aware of the love of his parents.'

'On rereading this account it appears as if motherhood is something of an endurance test (in those early months especially, it was!) Nevertheless, I cannot overstate the positive side of being a mum. There is nothing to compare with the joys and pleasures I have experienced through Andrew. Each day is different, often frustrating, always tiring, but there is so much fun and so much laughter.'

'Looking after him from birth has been rewarding, much more than I thought.'

'I feel that motherhood has given me more confidence to tackle other things in and out of the home environment and appreciate the companionship that a child gives to its mother, which is very special.'

'In the end my expectations, hopes, etc., have had to be modified by the reality of being a mother. The ideal is surely to find the balance that must exist between satisfying the needs of one's own children, of giving them love and security, and between the need to have one's own needs satisfied. And this is where my own expectations of being a good mother fall down, in that I've had to recognise a selfish streak in my nature and there are times when I feel like the child, with my own needs requiring satisfaction. I seem to have come full circle.'

This struggle to balance her needs and those of her child is very positive learning indeed. Unless we recognise the child within us we can't understand children or ourselves. There is nothing 'wrong' in having needs and wanting them to be met, and the struggle isn't about how to deny our needs but how to have them met without harming other people and preferably in such a way that someone else's needs are met simultaneously – often we deny others a needed opportunity to give because we can't bring ourselves to ask for what we need. Those of us who were brought up never to hurt other people, even if it meant denying our true feelings, find it difficult to distinguish between hurting and harming. There are times when we have to say what we feel, knowing that what we say may be hurtful, but if we want to go on growing and developing we can't endlessly shield ourselves or others from being hurt.

At the other end of the pendulum-swing some parents seem so determined not to deny their feelings and desires that they pursue their careers or higher education without pausing to consider that by doing so they may be lessening the chance of their own child developing towards his full potential. Some even feel that the state has a 'duty' to look after their children in view of their 'contribution to society'.

Then why have children? As 'an experience'? If the

baby is to provide the 'experience' then the parents have a particular obligation to see that in return his emotional as well as his physical needs are met in the early years. Given a good start in life, his later contribution to society may be of even greater value than his parents' present contribution.

It is never easy to balance our own needs with those of our children, but fortunately it doesn't all rest upon our conscious pre-natal decisions. Nature has evolved ways and means for young plants, animals and humans to get what they need for survival and their later development, as these two parents discovered:

'We waited for seven years before having a baby principally because we were satisfied with our professional, social and leisure life and realised that a child would alter things considerably.

'However, when we embarked on parenthood we were determined that the child would be permitted to change what is particularly important to each of us as little as possible, namely my continuing my profession as a veterinary surgeon and my husband dragging the whole family round the wilder parts of Europe in pursuit of his great love, ornithology. To a fair degree we both intended to try to ignore the advent of a baby during my pregnancy, which was an easy one. I continued to work three mornings a week until a fortnight before the baby was due. My husband did not attend any of the pre-natal classes which included husbands and I was very prickly about the ante-natal relaxation classes, feeling that afternoons of "baby-talk" were going to bore me.

'In fact I found those most useful, especially the actual relaxation exercises.

'My husband was reluctantly coerced into being present at the birth and was a tower of strength, literally taking over from the midwife during the final stages with his exhortations to "Push – now!"

'The hospital being overcrowded, I was discharged in seventy-two hours – then the panic set in. What were we going to do with this tiny, demanding creature. First nappy change took us both and still it wouldn't go on properly.

'The first six months were exhausting. Callum was on demand feeding and I didn't seem to have enough milk. We had never bargained before he was born just how strong the tie between mother and infant is, and no matter how exhausted that cry wakes you and forces you to go and see why.

'We have succeeded in our ambition not to let my career go nor our expeditions. When Callum was ten weeks old we took him sailing and touring to the Scottish Outer Hebrides, a year later to the Costa Doriana game reserve in southern Spain, and more recently touring in Provence in December. I returned to work part-time when he was three months old and have enjoyed my profession as never before, providing as it does an outlet from the domestic round.

'In conclusion I would say that our pre-baby thoughts that a child needn't be allowed to completely alter the way of life which is important to you, have proved correct. Also we have been delighted and astonished by the great love we have for him and he for us – completely confounding the rueful jokes before his arrival: "What if he/she doesn't really like me and I don't like him/her?" '

Surprises

'The idealistic view that one's influence and guidance would produce model children to form one's family was soon shattered by the emergence of such complete and independent characters so early in their lives.'

'My biggest surprise about toddlers is how much of a mind of their own they have. They decide on something they want and it's difficult to dissuade them. The strangeness of things that please them is also marked – the seventeen-month-old girl currently likes walking around carrying shapes from the post-box. They have their own patterns of sleep and feeding too that seem inbuilt, and trying to manipulate them usually ends in trouble.'

'Something that surprised me was how active he was at an early age, that he would pull the table cloths off the tables, pull out drawers and take out everything in them, and race around all day in his baby walker. We still have to wheel him to sleep in his pushchair. I thought you just put babies to bed and they would go to sleep after a hard day's play. I never realised that even young babies have a strong will of their own and that they can be disobedient.'

'. . . the pleasure of seeing Claire and Jamie develop, of seeing them get satisfaction from their achievements. I love seeing Claire's confidence and interest in other people and her desire to mix with them. Jamie is not so confident but I hope this will come with time. I think the trust and hope of children is quite remarkable and I feel there is so much we could learn from them. Their enthusiasm, as long as it is *their* enthusiasm, for following through interests and hobbies is catching.'

We can certainly learn from children, but parents need to make time to watch and listen if they are to learn, and sometimes need help to interpret and understand what they are seeing and hearing. Mother and toddler clubs and playgroups offer parents a unique opportunity to watch a variety of children at about the same *age* offering living proof that each is at a different *stage* – and that although each appears to be 'backward' in some skills and 'forward' in others this may be accounted for by the fact that 'backward' children are merely meeting a new skill for the first time.

Most parents need reassurance that their children are 'normal', but this can only come about as they begin to understand the wide range of 'normality'.

'I don't believe I thought much about life with children. I assumed they slept a lot, "cooed" and "gooed", cried when wanting a feed which could be easily satisfied – and later that tantrums and bad moods were more or less momentary. I assumed life would be most rewarding.

'My first child shattered all that. She seemed to need far less sleep than I did, she howled all day, and played all evening and far into the night, she dragged me from my bed at hourly intervals for months on end, and worst of all she never gave any return. As a baby I scarcely knew who she looked like, as she settled herself permanently over my shoulder; she never smiled or chattered, and I frequently felt she was deliberately trying to make my existence a misery! Fortunately in her late-night antics she was a joy to watch, but she acted always as a loner. She is now four, and a lovely little girl, but still persists in avoiding any approaches from me. The one thing I can do with her is read to her, which she loves, and would enjoy ad infinitum.

'The second baby is in complete contrast. From the start we have communicated perfectly, and the satisfaction and pleasure, particularly after the feelings of rejection by the first, has been wonderful. She has acted as a calming influence on the whole house, and made my relationship with the elder child improve greatly. My whole attitude to her is different as a result, and I thoroughly appreciate her and enjoy her.

'Besides the discovery that small children are, however easy they are to live with, extremely time-consuming, and delightfully messy and untidy beyond my wildest dreams, I have discovered that I know very little about them and the older they become, the less I seem to know. I have become 100 per cent more tolerant, and know that that needs to be doubled again, and have a sympathy which I never had before for people who molest and batter their children. I now know how frustrating and depressing they can be, and I have had none of the external pressures which so many people have.

'Above all, I have had far, far more pleasure from my two children than I could ever have imagined. I have had many delightful hours pottering behind them, wet, shivering, but fascinated to see them exploring, climbing, running, playing with pebbles, mud, water, and coming home mucky, happy and contented. I dread the day when they both go off to school!

'I think mothers-to-be need prior warning of the possible difficulties they could have. Preparation for birth is excellent, but no preparation for the all-important follow-up is given. I know I was convinced I had the worst baby on earth, and I had no means of discovering otherwise. Mothers with crying babies tend to avoid "troubling" other people, while what they need most is to realise that they are not alone and that it is not their fault! The opportunity to let off steam anywhere but on the baby – and I believe the baby is as sensitive to bottled-up feelings within the mother as to overt activities – can do wonders for the mother, and will probably greatly improve the baby's lot as well where the mother is less tense and as a result more able to appreciate its needs.'

Many mothers have experienced this rejection, and often don't even realise that there is anything unusual about it because it is their first relationship with a baby and they have no means of making a comparison. They often feel disappointed, hurt, baffled and frustrated and decide that motherhood is overrated, or feel guilty and blame themselves for being a failure as a mother, or feel angry with their baby for being so unrewarding. Many come through the experience to enjoy a good relationship with their child later on. A very small minority discover that they

34

have an autistic child who needs special help, whilst they themselves need the support of parents who have been through the experience before them. And some reach breaking-point and are violent in an attempt to win some response when every other approach has failed.

Before growing anxious, remember that some children are much more self-contained than others, some seem to be too busy to have time to spend on cuddles, and some just don't like being cuddled. Others are fiercely independent at one stage and warmly affectionate at others. If you are concerned about your child, then talk to your doctor or health visitor. If you are concerned about your feelings towards your child then there are the names and addresses of those who will help you, anonymously if you wish, at the end of the book.

The overall impression that I have from the letters is that there seems to be a need for post-natal gatherings, where new parents can talk and think about the ending of one stage of their lives. Endings and partings have their own natural sadness and it may be that unless this stage is recognised and lived through almost as a brief period of mourning it cannot be relinquished gracefully in order to start the new stage with hope, courage and realistic expectations.

Perhaps there is a pregnancy for parenthood that has its conception at the baby's birth (there is *no way* that parents can be prepared for this moment before it happens), and perhaps as much preparation and support is needed during the emotional nine months after birth as during the nine months before. At the moment it is as though a forceps delivery of 'instant parenthood' is expected both by the parents themselves and society in general.

Together with time and help to make their own emotional adjustment to this new phase in their lives, I think many parents would like to be a little clearer in their understanding of what it is reasonable, and unreasonable, to expect in the way of response from their toddlers. A great deal of distress is caused to both parents and children by false expectations, especially of a toddler's ability to understand, remember, obey, think (as we understand thinking) and reason. If only toddlers had been able to write letters saying what they thought it would be like to be born, and what it actually is like now that they have been in outer-space for a year or two!

The following section is an attempt to identify with toddlers' experiences and feelings as understandingly as we can identify with each other.

How it Feels to be a Toddler

Toddlers are not just small grown-ups, they are to adults rather as tadpoles are to frogs – one day tadpoles will be frogs but meanwhile they have the advantage of looking so different from their parents that no one expects them to be frog-like in their behaviour. Toddlers look so like small editions of ourselves that it is easy to overestimate their stage of development. They can sense far more than they understand, and when they respond to what they sense we tend to think that they have understood what we actually said, and therefore we begin to build up unrealistic expectations of their future behaviour.

If we call out sharply in our panic 'No! put that down, you'll hurt yourself' the child is likely to respond to our urgency by dropping whatever it was he was about to investigate. But it is quite possible that the words 'put that down' have no real meaning, especially if under normal circumstances we say 'No, give it to me' or 'No, don't touch' as we stretch out our hand to remove the object, and if the word 'down' is usually associated with 'down the road'.

Once we begin to assume that children understand the words we use we may jump to the conclusion that as soon as they can talk they will not only understand and respond but remember and reason as well. The connection between talking and understanding varies greatly from child to child, and remembering and reasoning comes later than we think.

Our placid first-born son said not a word until he was two, yet he seemed to understand and respond almost by telepathy from quite an early age. Our quicksilver daughter was equally slow to speak and she was so busy 'doing' that she never had time to listen to what was said, let alone to respond. Other children speak very much earlier: some prattle away just for the joy of being able to do so, but are better at talking than listening; others both talk and listen carefully. Whatever children's individual variations of speech and response, we almost always overrate the ability of young children to remember and to reason, and this is one of the chief causes of frustration between us.

If only we could understand what goes on in their minds life would be so much easier. As it is they put themselves or our possessions at risk, we put a stop to it and try to explain, they look at us with quivering lips and brimming eyes, or they throw their arms round us and give us kisses – then off they go to do exactly the same thing again. Do they forget so soon? Or do they remember, and decide that they are going to do it anyway? Do they do it deliberately to provoke us? Do they decide that even if we are cross they can soon wheedle us round afterwards? Surely, we think, they understood what we were saying. Why else would they have looked so sorry and tried to put things right between us? The chances are that they didn't understand all that we said but they responded to our tone and mood, and the upset between us mattered so much that the cause of it was forgotten – and is therefore likely to be repeated.

A great deal of research has been done to discover how children learn to think, but much of it is difficult to read let alone to understand in relation to our own children as we try to cope with them all day at home. It may help to try to put ourselves in a toddler's place and to look at his experience of his parents and home from his point of view. What follows will be fiction founded on fact, but sometimes it is justifiable to attempt an explanation in story form if the result helps to make matters a little clearer.

Forget for a moment how complex a human brain really is and try to imagine a newborn baby's brain to be rather like an empty storehouse lined with shelves and pigeonholes. Then try to picture a constant flow of images, sounds, tastes, smells and 'feels' flowing into the store-house through the baby's eyes, ears, mouth, nose and skin and whole nervous system. At first all these experiences flow in higgledly-piggledy and the baby isn't even aware that it is happening. Gradually a few constantly recurring ones begin to stand clear of the general unknowingness – parents and food are greeted with delight – but it is a long and puzzling process for a new human being to learn to recognise and to make connections between the hundreds of things that he sees, hears, smells, touches and feels every day.

The amount of learning that each of us acquired during our first two or three years is beyond our recall, but if we try to follow a child's learning related to an ordinary biscuit we may begin to sympathise with the enormity of the task ahead of him, especially if we remember that he is also learning a foreign language at the same time. Imagine that your very young crawler or toddler is on the rug while you scramble through the early evening tidying and cooking, and that in order to keep him peace-fully occupied you have given him a rich-tea biscuit (his very first biscuit of any kind) and a small wooden spoon. He won't even know that one can be eaten and the other can't. They are both the same colour but their shape is different, and he will probably pick up whichever one is nearest to him. He will reach out to grasp it, wave it about, bang it on the floor and even hit himself accident-ally, but eventually it is almost bound to go in his mouth. If it is the wooden spoon it may feel good against his gums, and he may suck and chew happily and ignore the biscuit. If it is the biscuit it may meet with his approval in a different way, and he will suck, break, bite and slowly devour those bits which don't end up as crumbs on the rug or a sticky mess down his front.

The next evening you may do the same again. He won't

be able to remember and recognise the two objects, and he will reach out for one of them at random as though he has never seen either of them before. If you repeat the process enough times then he *will* be able to recognise which one is the biscuit (which he will pick up and eat if he is hungry), and which one is the spoon (which he will pick up and brandish if he isn't hungry).

But suppose you decided on a change of biscuit and bought a packet of chocolate fingers, what then? How could he possibly look at a chocolate finger and recognise it as a biscuit? The colour, shape and size are all different and it is a totally new thing as far as he is concerned. He will have to go through the whole process of exploration again before he even discovers it is edible, let alone learns that this quite different looking thing is also called a biscuit.

Imagine that you work your way through all the varieties that you can buy, and that eventually he can recognise them all, what would he know about each of them? He might (but only just might, and it's stretching it a bit) be able to have some sort of memory that enables him to look at the chocolate ones with a vague recollection of brownness on his hands and clothes, and sweetness round his mouth and on his fingers afterwards. He just might be able to look at a ginger biscuit and recall a vague sensation of hurt at the corners of his mouth and on his tongue, and a sort of blinking feeling in his eyes, and a twitching in his nose. He just might be able to look at a cheese biscuit and half recapture the satisfaction of squeezing it in his fist, and then of loosening his fingers to release a drift of small white flaky pieces.

At this point if he could think clearly and put his thoughts into words (which he most certainly can't) he might say to himself: 'Good! The storehouse of my mind isn't such a muddle as it used to be. I have already put the memory of things I can eat on a shelf labelled 'Food', and now I suddenly see that a lot of things on that shelf that looked, tasted, felt, behaved and were named differently are in fact all members of one family called 'Biscuits'. So now I shall put all that information together neatly in a pigeonhole labelled 'Biscuits' on a special place on the 'Food' shelf. I wonder if I know enough about anything else to be able to gather it up and put it into another pigeonhole on another shelf?'

We might think that on the shelf marked 'Family' he could easily pigeonhole 'Dad'. But is it all that easy for a young child to assemble the assorted memories and experiences of his father? There is one man with a face with bristles that prick and another who is smooth; there is one man in pyjamas, another in light-coloured trousers and gay shirts, and another looking dark all over on rather special occasions. There is one who sings loudly, and one who croons gently when you wake crying in the night, and one who speaks in a dark-brown voice when you behave badly. There's another extraordinary and vast one who gets off his motorbike and you can't see that it's a person at all until the big round top-thing comes off.

But eventually, no matter what you wear, or do, or sound like, you will be recognised, even your tread on the stairs will be familiar, and the information will be gathered together and pigeonholed. In one way the store-house is becoming easier to use, but at the same time it is also becoming more complicated, for now there are times when the toddler discovers that he needs to use two pigeonholes at the same time, for example 'Mum' or 'Dad' and 'Biscuits'.

At tea time you and your toddler may sit up to the table together having tea and milk and biscuits, and everything is warm and lovely between you until something very odd happens from his point of view: you spoil it all by speaking in a cross voice, and the words you keep using are 'eat it nicely'. What is 'nicely'? After repeated experience it dawns upon him that it is not nicely if you are so hungry that you stuff your mouth full, or if you bang

41

your biscuit about until it disappears, or if the dog comes along and you want to drop it overboard and watch Fido eat it up.

Slowly he is learning, but it will be a very long time before he understands all this well enough to be able to work out that if he is starving he can either control himself, eat slowly, and be thought good, or eat quickly and put up with the consequences because it's worth it. For a long time yet he won't be able to control his immediate need to satisfy his hunger as quickly as possible and, when he does learn to control it, it will be because the happiness of tea time with you means more to him than the gobbling of the biscuit. He is beginning at last to be able to control the natural 'I want it now' stage.

Armed with his comfortable knowledge of what 'nicely' is all about he may one day discover the biscuit tin with the lid open. He can't possibly resist the biscuits once he has seen and smelled them, but he can and does remember the nicely bit, so he sits himself down on the floor by the tin and *very* nicely, one at a time and slowly, he eats a few. You come along, make fierce exclamations, jerk him up quite roughly, ram the lid on the tin, shut the door, remove him, and surely leave him thinking (only he can't yet think as we can) 'What on earth was that all about? I'm absolutely certain that I was sitting nicely, and eating nicely.'

However, eventually this experience too is understood and he files away one more piece of hard-earned knowledge into his biscuit pigeonhole (and also his mother and father pigeonhole); he is now clear that it simply isn't good enough to sit nicely and eat nicely – you have to combine the two as you sit on a chair at a table.

He's learning fast. That is, he was until the day you all went to the seaside. The sea was unexpected, so was all that sand, and it was good to have nice, safe, dependable parents there to make it all right, and what could be more reassuring than the call 'Dinner time'? But, horror of horrors, there was no table, and no chairs, and everybody was sitting on the ground – so was somebody going to be cross and spoil it all? Not a bit of it. Without a word of explanation everybody proceeded to eat a large lunch in the happiest atmosphere, and no one was sitting nicely at all, in fact Dad was almost lying down. Baffling!

The next learning concerns time. If he asks for a biscuit (nicely) he is given different answers at different times of the day: at 8.30 a.m. it is 'No'; at 10.30 it is 'No' (at home, but 'Yes' at Granny's); at 12.30 it is 'No'; at 4 it is 'Yes, and would you like another?' But at 6.30 when he is in bed, there is the most adamant 'No' of the lot, and this time it is something to do with teeth. (What have teeth got to do with it? The 'Teeth' pigeonhole only has unrelated snippets in it like brushes that sometimes touch where it hurts in your mouth; grandad's teeth in a glass; pink toothpasty spit trickling down the basin; tubes to squeeze. What has it got to do with biscuits?)

The learning still isn't over. If, at a stage when he is talking well and really understands the meaning of words like 'most' and 'same', you produce two identical packets of biscuits and open one and let him take all of them out and arrange them on a plate, and then say, 'Your biscuits are on the plate and mine are still in their packet. Who has the most?' his eyes would almost certainly tell him that he had the most. He wouldn't be ready to understand or accept your reasoning if you said, 'But your biscuits came out of a packet just like mine, so we must both have the same, mustn't we?' He has to believe the truth according to his eyes at this stage, because that is *his* truth.

There is still another stage of learning ahead. Imagine you have gone shopping and are walking home happily looking at this and that when you suddenly realise that the biscuits have fallen off the top of the basket. You know at once that all you have to do is retrace your footsteps until you find them. Your child (probably nearer schoolboy than toddler now) knows no such thing. He has to go, with all speed and considerable anxiety, straight back to where he last felt certain of seeing them, which is likely to be the shop. Once there he would be able to retrace the route with a marvellous precision, round this lamp-post twice, through that puddle, looking in this shop, standing on that manhole cover, until the packet was found. It will be later still before he can reverse a journey accurately. (Do some of us still find difficulty in reversing a car journey?)

Just think of all the learning that developed from that first sight of a biscuit, and remember that it all has to be repeated for every single object. Each time he has to learn:

What is the nature of this thing?

What can I do to it?

What can it do to me?

How will my mother react to me while I am doing all this learning?

Will my father react in the same way, or do I have to learn about two sets of reactions?

And that is only the first physical and emotional stage of his learning, before he knows the names of many of the objects or feelings associated with them, and long before he can be 'sensible' or 'good' or 'careful' according to our reasoning and experience.

What he needs is time, and this should be the one time in his life when there is time to give him time. Yet the pace of our lives is such that more often than we realise we say each day 'Hurry up! . . . Come along! . . . Quickly!'

Children live by development-time, we live by clock-time, and the two can be better synchronised once we begin to understand more about our toddlers and ourselves.

The Shock of Aggression

One of the most distressing aspects of aggression is the shock of its appearance, not just in our toddlers but in ourselves.

Many of us were brought up to believe that aggression is wrong, and from an early age we were taught to curb our natural instinct to hit, kick, bite, scratch, pull hair and throw things. Most of us hand this teaching on to our children in the belief that no one should hurt or intimidate others. But somewhere along the line confusion sets in and we come to believe that not only is it wrong to *be* aggressive, it is just as wrong to *feel* aggressive, and we try to stifle such feelings instead of admitting them and then trying to deal with the cause. We may even come to think that aggression is no longer part of our make-up, or else we acknowledge that it is still there but are confident that it is safely under control.

The greater our self-control, the more we deplore its lack in others. Every time a case of child battering hits the headlines people are appalled. If we are honest many of us who are genuinely appalled would have to admit that we can well understand how it happens, especially the once-only act of violence brought about by sheer exhaustion and desperation.

If we are to cope with aggression both in ourselves and in others we must first recognise that it is a right and proper part of us: parents will fight fire and flood to save their children's lives; men will fight boredom in a job to safeguard the pay packet on which their families depend; women will fight their physical and nervous exhaustion to look after their families; doctors and nurses fight for their patients' lives; so do the patients if the will to live is still there. We all try to attack problems, and obstacles and life itself because this is something we have also been taught to do, but it is called 'courage' or 'character' rather than 'positive aggression'. The last thing we should want to do is to eradicate aggression; we need to accept it and channel it in such a way that it becomes helpful instead of harmful.

If you are one of those parents who is shocked by the aggression that your toddler arouses in you, be comforted to know that you are not alone. If you are really frightened that you may harm your child, then seek help. But the chances are that you will be better able to cope with this phase of being a parent if you understand what is happening to you and your child.

After all the earlier uncertainties and adjustments of being a parent there often comes a period of particular pride and happiness and it is not unusual to hear parents say, 'We almost want him to stay as he is. He's as good as gold, cuddly, affectionate, goes to anybody, just never cries, and we haven't had a disturbed night for ages.' If you are one of these fortunate families you will hear on all sides how lucky you are to have such a placid child, but others will give you the credit for being good parents, and the truth probably lies somewhere between the two. The satisfaction is particularly gratifying if you are one of those who feel that this is the first time in your life that you have done something not just well but triumphantly.

And then, out of the blue, you suddenly seem to have a defiant obstructionist on your hands who loses no opportunity of refusing to cooperate, who wants his own way over everything, and who suddenly doesn't even want to be cuddled. You are pushed aside literally and metaphorically, and as the shock of it sinks in you say to yourself 'What have I done? Where did I go wrong?' and there seems to be no answer.

You have probably tried everything you can think of and nothing works. One neighbour says he is getting spoilt and you ought to be firm and put a stop to it (this doubles the number of daily upsets). Another says that you should take no notice and the phase will pass (how can you take no notice when the upsets are wearing you both out?). The grannies are concerned for you all, but baffled, because memories grow rosy with age and they truly think they mean it when they say that neither you nor your husband was ever like that (don't believe a word of it).

The health visitors and clinic staff could reassure you, but by this time you have probably stopped attending because everything seemed plain sailing once he was walking, talking, eating and sleeping well. If you had talked with such people they could have prepared you for the next stage; they could have explained that precisely because you have been good parents your child is strong, healthy, happy, secure, intelligent and normal in the fullest sense of that comfortable word. The pride and pleasure of a job well done would have braced you for the news that precisely because he was all these things the next stage would be for him to dare to develop his own personality rather than endlessly bask in the warmth of yours.

You may well remember the same thing happening between you and your parents, particularly if you were a close and loving family. There probably came a time when there was a strong urge to sort out what *you* felt and wanted from what you felt *they* felt and wanted from you. You wanted to be yourself, not their shadow and echo.

So it is with your toddler, and once you see the tears and tantrums not just as a personal family crisis but as part of a wonderfully natural cycle of human growth and development, then the worry, frustration and guilt will lessen, leaving you in a better position to cope with this particularly wearing phase. Meanwhile, try to put yourself in your toddler's place to see if you can sense how he may be feeling.

Imagine how you might feel if you were spirited away to a land of giants. The adults in your new world would be between ten and eleven feet tall; table tops would be above your head, chair seats at chest level; car door handles would be head-height, dogs the size of lions, and horses the size of elephants; buses would be equivalent in height to four-decker buses; the names of roads, in a language you couldn't read, would be above your head; front-door keyholes would be hopelessly out of reach, and in any case the intricate system of opening them would be unmanageable; shop counters would be above your head, and you would be imprisoned in a forest of legs unable to see what you wanted to buy, unable to hand over money, unable to comprehend the whole system of money.

If you were lost, how would you know which gigantic house, in which nameless street, was your home? In the giant's home the light switch would be out of reach, and darkness would stay dark. The oven, big enough for you to get inside, would stay cold although you knew it was miraculously capable of becoming hot. Large jars and packets in the cupboard would line towering shelves – but what was the connection between those cold and unfamiliar things, the heat of the oven, and delicious hot food on the table?·

In short, you would not only feel but also *be* frighteningly helpless and inadequate to survive in this new land if the giants in charge of you did not remain constantly near at hand and ever willing to go on being in charge of you. No wonder children fear being lost, or left alone, or being deserted by their own personal giants.

Consider further. Your giant takes you out for a walk, and meets another giant, and they jabber away to each other, their voices floating down from ten feet or so above ground level. Suddenly you hear your name, and begin to listen intently. And there is your beloved giant telling someone how you wet the bed again, and about what you did yesterday that caused such an upset. How *could* she tell about those things? Is nothing safe between you? Then both giants look down, and the strange one talks in an unnatural voice and says things about being a naughty boy – and there have you been standing like a pillar of virtue while they betrayed you up above!

Consider one step further. Suppose you have been driven by instinct to rebel against your personal giants, how would you feel if they stopped being warm and friendly and in control of you and the world around you? Or if one became very fierce nearly all the time while the other went to the opposite extreme when the fierce one was out of the way? It is better to have two united giants, either too strong or not strong enough, than to be bewildered between two extremes, for that would teach you to play one parent off against the other and this is a game where all the players are losers.

Your toddler wants and needs to test his surroundings and his relationships but he needs to know that as he experiments you are still strong and caring enough to set certain limits and to keep him safely within them. Once you begin to understand that although he needs to be free enough to dare to be outrageous he still needs to know that you are stronger than he is, then you can quietly rethink the overall situation and make a plan of campaign. You can't plan the battles but at least you can view the lie of the land, assess your strengths and weaknesses, and note the places where you feel battles would be fought on poor ground.

Your weaknesses are likely to be that:

1   You have lost confidence, but this will begin to come back if you realise that this phase is not your 'fault' but a natural stage of growth and development.
2   You are afraid to be really firm in case you dominate and thwart your child's personality. Your viewpoint may be different once you see that none of us can discover and develop our true personalities without guidelines and certain set limits in the early years.
3   You are physically and emotionally worn out. This

can be improved by allowing yourself a period when you are kind to yourself, and a few early nights may help as well if you can get them.

4   Your perspective is probably impaired and you may be living from battle to battle without seeing the whole stage of development of which the battles are but a part.

5   You may suffer from pre-menstrual tension if you are a mother, or pressures at work if you are a father or a working mother, so decide at once that you will avoid clashes on those days. This is not weakness, it is common sense.

6   You may fear that you will be too much of a moral coward to take decisive action, or that you will try to take it but fail – and that is probably what frightens you more than anything else. If you are a father your upbringing may have so stressed 'kindness to women and children' that you may be afraid to be 'strong', or even afraid that you will hurt your child when you don't mean to just because you are physically strong.

Your strengths are almost certainly that:

1   You love your child and truly want to do your best for him.

2   You may now have a better understanding of just why he needs you to be able to say 'No' and mean it when occasion demands.

3   Your love and growing understanding for your child, and the support of those who have been through it all before you, will almost certainly enable you to discover that you have reserves of moral courage, strength, patience and ability that amaze you.

4   You have caught the situation in time.

5   The very fact that you are beginning to think positively instead of feel negatively will bring a measure of calm.

The first stage of coping with the situation is to try to avoid clashes as far as possible for a while, before the dreaded 'No' becomes a habit for both of you. If it has been 'No' to the breakfast egg lately, then settle for cereals and toast, or milk, or whatever is on the breakfast table (no, not chocolate cake just because he demands it) and let him have his protein in another form at another meal.

It bears repeating, try to avoid *unnecessary* conflict, particularly if you are aware that your instinct is to bring every issue to a head in order to be sure that you can still 'win'. You are right to feel that he mustn't have his own way over everything, but since there are some issues that really do need firmness on your part it is both wise and generous to give in gracefully over the bids for independence that really are permissible. If he wants to sleep with his head at the foot of the bed, then does it matter? You can probably remember doing this yourself, and the feeling of excitement and strangeness that accompanied the changed view of the room.

Another point to bear in mind at this stage is that every time you ask a question you are offering a direct invitation to say the magic word 'No'. The once innocent 'Shall we get ready for our walk now?' is likely to be met by 'No. I don't want to go for a walk', so change the formula to 'I am going to make some cakes for tea tomorrow so when we are out we must buy some currants and some sultanas.' This takes the emphasis off the shall-we-shan't-we short-term decision by creating an interest beyond. This may sound like the giving-in of moral cowardice, but really it is meeting him half way: what you are trying to convey to him is that until now you have both mostly done things *your* way, but now you recognise that sometimes he wants to feel big and strong and important enough to have things done *his* way.

Sometimes he will still have to fall in with your decisions, but sometimes you can quite properly fall in with his. You will find yourself having to rethink some of your

51

ideas of what is 'proper', but this sort of self-questioning is essential if we are to go on growing up ourselves. If he wants to go shopping wearing the tea cosy, what is your reaction? Will other people laugh at you? Or not notice? Or notice with amusement and understanding? Or laugh with your child and admire you for being able to carry it off as the natural impulse that it is? Only you know whether you could allow it, but be honest with yourself as to your real reasons.

Once your child feels that there is give and take the aggressive phase often passes without being unduly wearing, but this sort of flexibility must never be confused with the damaging attitude of 'Oh well, anything for a quiet life!' If you find that the demands are growing more and more outrageous, then you will sense that the time has come to take firmer and more positive steps for everyone's sake – but to do this you need to think ahead as to how you might tackle the crunch when it comes.

No one can tell you what to do, for only you know what feels right for you and your child at any given time. Ask other people what they do, and see if among the widely different answers that you are likely to be offered there are one or two suggestions that sound helpful and which would still enable you to be true to yourself.

Some may say that one really good smack worked for them. You may know at once that this could never be right for you; or you may have been driven to it already only to discover that it didn't work for either of you; or, although you have never done such a thing before, you might be prepared to try it if nothing else works; or you might fear that, in the words of one mother, 'I knew if I hit him I'd go too far.'

Some may shut their child in another room until he calms down. You may be fearful about what he would do alone in a room, or you may have memories of being shut in a room that recall real fear, or you may have felt when you were released that nothing had been resolved, or you may think it would be a good idea to remove the child from a family gathering or his upset friends but to stay with him until he is calm and you can return together.

There is no 'right' way. All the above methods have worked for some parents and children but not for others. Bribery is never the right answer because it leads to 'blackmail', though most of us have been tempted to use it as a delaying tactic in a moment of weakness under extreme pressure in embarrassing circumstances. But it is a sign that we are at the crossroads and have to decide who is going to be the one to win the next show-down, and how.

The way that works best for me is to wait for a crisis of screaming defiance, or floor-bashing prostration, and then to pick the child up and hold him firmly under one arm with his legs kicking harmlessly in the air behind and his two flailing hands held firmly in my free hand (kept well away from gnashing teeth). At this stage the child is rather like a vigorous swimmer with the buoyant safety of a life-belt encircling him: he is stranded and helpless yet feels safely held, literally and metaphorically.

A child can continue kicking and screaming for a surprisingly long time, and this is physically tiring and hard on the ears and nerves. According to his weight it may be easier to pace up and down or to stand firmly with feet planted wide apart rocking him rhythmically, and if the noise begins to get inside my head and threatens to disturb my calmness (which is essential) then I sing a nursery rhyme to myself. It needs so little concentration that my attention is not distracted from the child, yet it distracts me just enough to ensure that I shall not become het-up myself. Eventually the screams turn to sobs and I drop into the nearest chair, swing him round from my hip to my lap, and rock him quietly until he is still enough to be comforted by the repetitive refrain: 'It's all right . . . it's all right . . . it's all over . . . it's all right.'

This is not the moment for a moral lecture or an ultimatum along the lines of '*Now* put away those toys'. The major battle has been won, and the proof is there in the relationship between you that it really is possible to love the sinner but not the sin. This time he knows that he will not be permitted to go beyond a certain point, and also that even when he is at his impossible worst you will not withdraw your love from him.

After I have bathed his face and given him a drink the child will indicate what is appropriate between us so I try to take my cue from him. Some children need to sleep; some like to pretend that nothing has happened and of their own free will go back to put the toys away; some go off with a favourite possession, but avoid the spot where the crisis began; and some just want us to stay quietly together for the rest of the day. If he stays as close as my shadow for several days I take it as a sign that he still feels a bit shaken by the violence of his outburst, and still needs reassurance that the lovely new relationship between us isn't too good to be true.

This method may work for you or it may not. You may not even want to try, or you may never need it at all, or you may want to try it but feel unready. Do nothing until you have had time to think about it, but if you do decide to try it then choose the occasion carefully: it is easier in your home than in a shop, easier alone than with an audience, easier when you are not overtired, easier when there is time ahead to see it through in its entirety. Above all it is easiest when you can say to yourself, 'I'm ready. The next time he heads for a crisis I shall see it coming and know that for both our sakes I can see it through with him.'

You and your child may well escape the stage of persistent tantrums, or you may experience it with one child but not another. If you do experience it, it may be a single continuous phase of frequent tantrums building up to a climax that leaves him knowing just how far he can go with you, after which there may be no more real difficulty on this score until the adolescent stage of rebellion. Or your particular child may go through fairly regular cycles of build-up and blast-off. I well remember one such child whose cycle seemed to be a fairly regular one of six weeks, and once this was seen as her pattern at that stage it was easier to see and understand the build-up and to be ready for the crisis when it came. It was also easier to accept without undue emphasis on the causes of the outburst, much as some women learn to recognise, accept and plan round the menstrual cycle as far as possible.

But in addition to all the underlying causes of development and temperament you will almost certainly have become aware of circumstances that trigger the occasional tantrum in almost any child.

The simplest and most frequent cause is probably being overtired. Which of us can't remember our own parents allowing us to stay up late for some treat, and then saying 'Bed! No, no later because you'll only be grumpy tomorrow'? I can remember throwing tantrums, and then being doubly furious when my parents looked at each other over my head and spelled out knowingly 'O–V–E–R–T–I–R–E–D'. I can even remember the occasion when something clicked as this mumbo-jumbo was chanted and I screamed, 'I am *not* overtired!'

There are bound to be occasions when children are overtired, and we learn by trial and error that if we add overexcitement then the effect is intensified. Most of us have tickled a fretful child and made him smile, then laugh, so we continue, and the laughter grows louder, and then suddenly he is over the top and grows hysterical. Again our parents' words come back to us: 'That's enough, it will only end in tears.'

Another cause can be apprehension or real fear. Can you remember seeing well-meaning parents trying to coax a child into the sea? The child is understandably reluctant in the face of such vastness, the shock of cold water, and the strange feeling under his feet and round his ankles as the water surges up and then pulls back, sucking the firmness away from under him. The parents don't want him to miss an experience that they feel he will enjoy once he is used to it, or they feel that their timid youngster is showing them up badly in front of the parents of bolder children, so they start to call out more urgently 'Come on! It's lovely!' and simultaneously they may begin to splash him – or even to pick him up, wade out and dunk him up and down. Would we like to be pushed out of an aeroplane into a vast sky with a hearty voice telling us that parachuting is lovely?

It is prevention rather than cure that is needed for a tantrum that is a primitive way of saying 'Don't, please don't . . . I don't know what it is . . . it's too big . . . too cold . . . it's alive and grabbing at my feet . . . I was happy on the sand, and looking at the sea from a safe distance . . . *Don't make me!*' So don't make him. There isn't any hurry, there isn't any sense in forcing a child against his instinct. Build up his confidence gently in *his* time and the chances are that his moment of readiness for the new experience will come quite naturally.

Another cause is the shock of hurt and surprise that heralds jealousy. A first child is the centre of his parents' world, and it is understandable that an influx of friends or relations can give him the disconcerting feeling that he doesn't matter any more. Anything is better than being ignored, and a howl of anguish and anger is often the spontaneous reaction. This is often met with unfeeling laughter and a cry of 'Whose nose is out of joint?', which makes things worse. Common courtesy can often prevent this happening: whether we are guests or host and hostess no one in the room should ever be left out of things for so long that they feel discomforted – any more than they should be allowed to monopolise attention. One helpful way of making a child feel important without becoming the centre of attention is to give him jobs to do that

will be helpful to others; then he can enjoy being person-
ally thanked as a bonus. If he is happy to be parted from
you he can show people where to put their coats or
shopping bags, ask each one if they would like a cup of
tea while you put the kettle on, carry round the sugar or
biscuits, take people upstairs to the bathroom – and show
them his bedroom, which will be good for a few minutes'
morale-boosting attention.

The advent of a new baby can be infinitely more upsetting because the guest doesn't go, and not only is his
mother's time and attention monopolised to an unwelcome
degree but often trusted friends and relations seem to
relegate him to second-best position. However eager we are
to see the new baby it really is very insensitive and
discourteous to ignore our former small friend and rush
to the pram saying 'May I see . . .?' If the pram and its
contents are ignored, and the friendship with the first-
born is re-established, then he may be the one to volunteer
the information 'We've got a new baby'. If he doesn't,
rather than pretend the momentous event in his life hasn't
happened it is sometimes helpful to say eventually, 'I
hear you've got a new baby, will you show me?' Even
then he needs to know that you are looking at the baby
together rather than to sense that you have switched off
him and on to the baby.

One rising-four-year-old expressed his mixed feelings
very clearly. A neighbour watched him guarding the
pram in the garden like a soldier, marching up and down
with his gun on his shoulder like a palace guardsman.
Then he drooped a bit, and finally stood looking at the
pram. Then he gave it a hefty kick. What could be a
clearer way of saying 'I know I ought to love and look
after you, but sometimes I hate the sight of you'?

History doesn't relate what happened next, but it may
have been one of two things. If the mother saw the incident through the window she might have rushed out,
grabbing him fiercely and pulling him away from the

pram, saying, 'You're a naughty boy, you might have tipped the pram over.' Or she might have gone out calmly saying, 'It's all right, you haven't hurt her, and you did guard her for a very long time didn't you? She's still asleep so let's go indoors and have a nice time together until she wakes up.' Jealousy compounded by guilt is a very uncomfortable state of mind. He can't cope with his feelings alone, and needs praise for everything he does that is commendable, and periods when he has his parents' undivided love and attention if he is to regain his confidence and peace of mind. And you, too, need somebody's undivided love and attention occasionally, someone to talk to who will understand exactly how tired, angry, baffled, worried and fed up you are sometimes. As one mother wrote, 'One thing for sure, it does help to talk or even write about them [harassing moments] – I feel better when things are out in the open!'

Part 2
The Doings of Toddlers

Over a hundred years ago the great educator Froebel wrote: 'Play is not trivial, it is highly serious and of deep significance. Cultivate it, and foster it, oh Mother. Protect and guide it, oh Father.'

As part of this protection and guidance, and in the deep belief that close proximity to nature was important to children, he devised and established kindergartens – literally special gardens for children.

Froebel wanted children to have first-hand experience of sand, clay, water, wood, stones, trees, grass, flowers, birds, insects and animals. He wanted them to be free to touch and manipulate, dig, build, climb, throw, run and rest. He wanted them to develop their curiosity and capacity to see, touch, listen, taste and smell. He wanted them to develop an awareness of beauty and wonder, a sense of responsibility, and the ability to solve problems. He wanted them to have reverence for life and an awareness of the universe.

Where better to learn all these things, he believed, than in a specially prepared garden that would give children the freedom to explore and extend themselves through play.

I think he would be sad to see how his wide vision has been narrowed down to the point where we seem to assume that modelling clay on a table is better than mud pies in the garden, that a water-tray is better than a bath or gumboots and a puddle, that a climbing frame is better than a tree. Often what we offer to children in nursery schools, playgroups and homes are small-scale substitutes for the real thing, better than nothing but still only substitutes. We are right to offer them, but should take every opportunity to give the natural experience whenever it is possible.

I think he would also be sad to see how his advice to cultivate, foster, protect and guide play is coming down so heavily on the 'guidance' that it often becomes interference, an interruption of concentration, and a cutting short of the repetition of experiences that is an essential part of play. Children need to go fully through each stage of development before going on to the next one, and there is great wisdom in the old country saying 'If you 'urry 'em forrard you'll backen 'em'.

Play is preparation for living, not just passing the time, or keeping them quiet, or getting them ready for school. Each day is an opportunity to discover something new, to learn how to do things, to find out where limits are set, to feel a wide range of emotions, and to go to bed with the tiredness of deep satisfaction. And at the end of every such day if dads come home in time for the goodnight kiss and say 'What have you been doing today?' the answer that sums up the whole day of living will be 'I've been playing'.

Remember this when encyclopedia salesmen call, or when you feel under pressure to buy 'educational toys', or to teach your baby to read, or even to add to the toy cupboard that is already full – the continual cry 'I've got nothing to play with' can't be satisfied with toys alone but by play which is doing and being, watching and copying, genuinely helping with real jobs and messing about, and day-dreaming.

The thought of Froebel in his garden with the children is delightful and has the ring of truth that we would do well to remember, but I also suspect that there was someone in the background who called out at intervals 'Your meal is ready', that he put on clean clothes without wondering how they made the transition from the dirty clothes basket to the drawers, and that he enjoyed relaxing at the end of the day in a room that seemed to keep itself clean, tidy and inviting.

Most toddlers are looked after by their mothers during the week, and by mothers and fathers together at week-ends, but this usually means that mother and child are shut up together for five days without relief from each other, and that the mother is constantly trying to balance

62

the counter-claims of the toddler, the home, her husband and herself.

Looking back to those days I have the impression that I was endlessly saying 'What are you doing?' in a slightly anxious voice when they were quiet and out of sight, or 'What are you doing *now*?' in exasperation as I beheld the latest outrage, or 'What shall we do now?' in happy companionship as we finished one job and contemplated the next. Of one thing I am certain, the toddler stage for me was characterised by *doing*. All day long they were busy doing this and that, pottering here and there, endlessly busy to no apparent purpose – one quietly and methodically, the other like a wound-up clockwork toy.

At the time I couldn't see their endless doings from their point of view because I was so stretched and strained from my point of view, and all my knowledge of child development seemed to apply only to other people's children. But now I see other parents feeling as I once felt and hope that I may be able to offer some insight into these 'doings', for they are actually play.

What they do may at first seem pointless but their reasons for doing it spring from needs that are really very understandable – especially when we recognise that we continue to have many of these needs ourselves, and often meet them in much the same way.

Since living with a toddler is a new experience to the vast majority of parents it seems sensible to start with the aspect of children's endless activity that is the most distressing for most parents, that of danger and destruction.

Destruction

It would be in keeping with the following sections to head this one 'Destroy and Create', but it would raise false hopes and expectations because at the toddler stage it is so natural and easy to destroy and so difficult to create.

We can all recognise how very much easier it is to break things than to mend them – one wind too many, and the watch's mainspring is broken; one jolt of the arm, and a stitch is dropped to run down to create havoc in an intricate knitting pattern; one slip of the chisel, and the woodcarving is spoilt; one quick movement of a wet hand and a treasured dish is in smithereens on the floor.

Very small errors of judgement can lead to repercussions out of all proportion, and these errors are particularly prevalent at the toddler stage because toddlers still have so little judgement, such undeveloped skills, so little knowledge of the consequence of their actions, and such an abundance of curiosity.

Although some children are careful, gentle and placid by nature it is really wisest for us, and fairest to them, to accept that this is an exceptionally destructive phase. Once this is accepted it is easier to keep calm and to tackle the problem in two ways, by prevention and by offering legitimate outlets for their natural destructive tendencies.

Prevention (of Destruction and Potential Self-destruction)

One father summed it up when he said 'We had puppies before children so we were used to the stage of putting everything out of reach, only with Jane at least we didn't have to put shoes and slippers on the mantelpiece.'

Many toddlers are so much more active and inquisitive

than parents anticipate that it really does pay to spend time and thought on putting things out of sight and reach, even to the extent of changing the contents of drawers and cupboards so that he finds dusters and brushes where formerly he might have found glass bottles of cleaning fluids and electric light bulbs. It also pays to put cereals and soap powders into plastic containers with finger-proof lids. The packets tip over so easily and the trodden contents are wasteful and time-consuming to sweep up.

Any ornaments or bits and pieces of intrinsic or sentimental value are best put right away at this stage, or else well out of reach – scissors, too, not only for safety but because it is devastating to discover an engrossed toddler happily cutting the hem of long curtains. Saucepan and frying-pan handles should all be turned so that they don't protrude over the edge of cookers, and for extra safety you may like to consider fitting safety guards which adjust to the top of most cookers.

All medicines should be stored out of reach, preferably in a specially designed safety cabinet. Fireguards need mesh tops as well as sides, and should be capable of being fixed to the wall. Safety gates at the top and bottom of stairs give extra peace of mind, as do childproof fastenings on any gate leading into the road.

All doors are a source of painful accidents. It is so easy to open a door quickly without realising that the toddler is behind it, or pull a door shut on leaving a room without seeing that the toddler's fingers are going to be trapped at the hinge-edge. If your door handles are low the toddler himself will sometimes shut a door and slam it on to the fingers of his other hand because he hasn't yet learned to anticipate where the door will be in relation to his fingers when it is shut. Car doors can be even more dangerous because most of us are in the habit of slamming them, and the metal edge can cut as well as bruise. Indoors it is a draughty but good precaution to make a 'sausage' with a loop at each end to slip over the handles on either side of each door. The filling needs to be firm enough to prevent the door closing, and the gap needs to be wide enough to ensure that even if fingers are where they shouldn't be they won't be squashed.

If you have an old house make sure that the electrical sockets are of the required safety type, and plug covers are a useful extra protection. Older houses often have hearth kerbs or raised brick hearths which although safely protected by the guard when the fire is alight can be tripped over when the guard is removed in the summer. One of the long snake-type draught excluders, rush matting squares joined in strips, or a mat can be a sensible precaution at the bumbling-about stage. Sharp edges and corners on low tables are also a hazard if a tumble will result in an injury at eye or head level.

All these precautions to protect the toddler from injury or even accidental self-destruction are part of the responsibility of being a parent and are accepted as such. It is more difficult to accept the sort of destruction that leads us to say in despair 'He just leaves a trail of wreckage behind him wherever he goes, he bangs, bites, tears, breaks, upsets or takes to pieces everything he can get his hands on!'

Children vary very much in their destructive tendencies, and parents' attitudes to destruction vary just as widely. You may be a warm-hearted, happy-go-lucky household where almost anything goes. You may have decided that it is no good trying to have a beautiful home while the children are young, and anyway your spending priorities may put house decoration and furnishings low on the list. Your children are likely to have ample opportunities for energetic and messy play, but remember that most children need somewhere cosy and peaceful in which to be cuddled up sometimes, and be tolerant if one of your children has a need to be meticulously tidy. Be watchful, too, in other people's homes for it is distressing to those who value their homes in a different way if a visiting child charges in and proceeds to clamber all over the furniture and uses the armchairs as trampolines.

On the other hand, you may have gone to great trouble to create a beautiful home before the children arrived, and they may well respond to their environment by being unusually appreciative and careful. But be watchful to keep the balance between your high standards and your children's need for freedom to develop through real playing in all its stages. One tragic case stays in my mind of a family so houseproud that they inserted glass panels into the drawing room door so that the children could kneel on the hall carpet and watch the television through the glass without damaging the room.

Yet less extreme forms of planning can work very well and many parents keep one room as they want it, shutting it up firmly unless the whole family is there together, whilst the rest of the house is 'just comfortable'. Other families keep the whole house 'reasonable' and give one room (if accommodation makes this possible) to the children, in which they can do as they like from an early age. Other families like a happy medium consistently throughout the house. The point is that you must be clear in your own minds about what constitutes damage and destruction.

Your own upbringing and temperament will have influenced you and you may be reproducing a happy family pattern, or you may be deliberately rejecting it in favour of something different, or you may have chosen a partner whose upbringing and temperament are in contrast to your own, in which case you may have reproduced the best of both worlds, or there may be conflict over some issues such as the casualness of one jarring on the carefulness of the other. You are as you are; but it would be sad to pass on habits of thinking and behaviour without examining them carefully in relation to the needs of each child you bring into the world, who needs to go through all the natural and necessary stages of development if he

67

is to be the happy and successful person you want him to be.

This opportunity to go on learning and to modify your own attitudes in the light of what you learn about children, and from your own child, is one of the great contributions that children make to the quality of your own lives.

Our concern during the destructive phase of growing-up is a natural one, as natural as the phase itself, but there is a great deal that can be done to lessen the damage, anxiety and exasperation. The destruction of toys can be particularly distressing, especially when parents look back to their own childhood and remember how few and treasured toys were, usually only received on birthdays and at Christmas.

Toy buying is still difficult for most parents, for the well established firms who really do understand the needs of children have few shops through which they sell directly to the public. At the moment most parents are limited to a small range of toys in the local corner shop, or to toyshops where the array is wide but guidance is not always available as to what constitutes a good buy at various stages.

The question of stage is all-important. Small replicas of cars are a great joy to children old enough to recognise the make and type of vehicle, but it is disappointing to give a toddler a miniature car only to find that he strips off and throws away the loose parts. It isn't really his fault: he doesn't see the tyres as tyres, his fingers just busy themselves exploring the small object and they work on anything movable until it is dismantled – and then he drops it in order to free his hands to explore further.

Little cars are greatly loved and it is a question of finding the right car for the right stage of play. Tonka make a range that are virtually indestructable. The smallest models are about 102 mm and are made of strong, colourful plastic and come in about eighteen different models. The larger models are about twice that size and are made basically of steel, strongly constructed with no sharp edges, have non-toxic rust- and chip-resistant surfaces, and have tyres which are made to last. The steel models are expensive, but both are excellent play value for years beyond the toddler stage.

The choice of toys during this destructive phase is particularly important, for if unsuitable toys are given then invariably they break and the child comes to believe that this is inevitable and nothing to be bothered about, and you are tempted to feel that he is careless and destructive. Strong, well designed toys give you value for money, and your child hours of satisfying play and a growing confidence in his ability to handle things safely and competently.

There are also occasions for short-term treats, and many of us will remember the joy of small windmills on sticks, little kittens that move when a bulb is squeezed, monkeys that climb up ladders, flags to stick in sand-castles, flowers that grow out of shells when they are immersed in glasses of water, balloons and bubble-blowing. None of these things is likely to have a very long life, but if this is known in advance then the ephemeral joy can be relished to the full while it lasts.

Legitimate Outlets

Children need and enjoy physical acts of destruction, and banging and tearing are high on the list. There are many ways to provide toddlers with a chance to do these things. Wooden hammer toys have excellent play value, and a good hearty bashing they can certainly stand. Clay and dough can also stand unlimited slapping, punching, poking, pinching, wringing and pulling apart by hand; they can also be hit, rolled, jabbed and bored by small wooden rolling-pins or the wooden hammer from the hammer toy. All these movements are necessary if fingers and wrists are to grow strong and the more his hands are used the more satisfied the toddler will feel. There is immense satisfaction in using our hands at any age and we only have to have a bandaged finger to realise how we miss, and didn't consciously appreciate, the freedom to handle things.

Tearing can also become a legitimate form of play. Just think of all the paper you screw up and throw in the waste-paper basket: paper bags, tea packets, cereal boxes, several layers of different papers from packets of biscuits, newspaper, envelopes. Rubbish to us, but each one so different in colour and texture for a toddler, and many of them go through a stage of enjoying being given the various papers to tear up into small pieces and drop into the waste-paper basket.

A small plastic bowl can be coated inside with Polycell and a toddler can spend a very happy, if sticky, time sitting on the floor with the bowl between his legs tearing paper, dropping it in, poking it about and tearing again. It takes only a few moments to soak it off ready for the next time.

Picture-making from torn paper comes at a much, much later stage. All you are doing at this stage is offering your toddler a legitimate way of tearing paper and the sticking is just to make it more interesting still, which will encourage him to tear yet more paper until he has done all the tearing that he wants to do at this stage.

Tearing and crushing on a much larger scale can be done on big cardboard cartons which most corner shops or supermarkets will be delighted to give you. At first they will be fun to get in, or to put things in, but as they grow flabby small tears will inevitably appear and at that stage the toddler can be invited to tear it all up (if he hasn't done it for himself already) and help you to put it in the dustbin. This last bit is important because slowly he needs to learn that we look after things as carefully as we can, mending them or cleaning them as necessary,

70

but that there are some things that we can tear up and throw away as rubbish, and that one lot of rubbish has to be cleared up satisfactorily before we create any more.

Slowly, very slowly, he will learn what he can tear and what he can't; what he can slap, bang and pinch and what he can't. He won't always keep to the rules, but at least he will come to know when he is doing something that he shouldn't whereas at the toddler stage so often he doesn't understand, can't remember, and can't control his impulses.

The stages of growth can't be hurried, but we can help immeasurably by providing opportunities for destructive play in an atmosphere of approval.

In and Out

Every parent knows the anxieties of the stage when everything within reach is put straight into the baby's mouth.
This is difficult enough, but once he can toddle the range
of objects that are sucked, bitten and chewed multiplies
alarmingly and the continual cry is 'Ugh! Nasty! Take
it out!', followed by a wail of despair to returning dads
in the evening: 'Honestly, you can't take your eyes off
him for a second. Today he's had in his mouth the soapy
flannel in the bath, the dog's bone, the handle of my
handbag, a banana in its skin, his shoe lace, a clothes peg,
the pencil by the telephone, and then the standard lamp
flex. That really scared me. If his teeth had gone through
could he have been electrocuted?' (If the wall switch had
been on, and the flex one of the old rubber-covered ones,
then indeed a live wire in a wet mouth would have caused
a severe shock – and an electric fire flex could be fatal.)

You long to be told that the phase will pass, but I'm
not sure that it ever really does pass. Do you still put
into your mouth, almost without knowing, cigarettes,
sweets, chips, bits of this and that each time you go into
the pantry, the left-over crusts from breakfast and tea,
blades of grass picked as you walk through the meadow,
or chewing-gum?

It's best really to accept that there is always a certain
satisfaction about chewing, sucking and eating at any
age. A teething toddler may revert to putting everything
in his mouth because he isn't able to curl his tongue round
to massage the spot that irritates or hurts, or even to rub
it with his finger. Try to think of something that might
help him – a raw scraped carrot to bite on or fingers of
bread baked hard in a low oven. These are cheap and
since it is the feel rather than the taste that matters you
will be meeting his need without creating an artificial
liking for sweet things.

Sometimes offering food is inappropriate, but there is still the need to bite on something hard. Plastic is cheap and hygienic. A small plastic container can be kept handy containing a selection of some of the earlier teething toys (but look at these carefully, for some that were suitable for front teeth won't go comfortably to the later trouble-spots further back in the mouth). The cooking utensil department of shops is a useful place to look; plastic measuring spoons or small wooden spoons with smooth handles may be helpful, but be sure that anything you buy is non-toxic and that it won't break or splinter.

As they grow older children tend to put things in their mouths less and less, but they still love to put things into things, so keep your eyes open for suitable receptacles. Try nice, firm, willow shopping-baskets, plastic pails with lids, old handbags, tall plastic dirty-clothes baskets (which will hold toys at bedtime), a metal teapot with its lid, cardboard cartons from the grocer, waste-paper baskets, or tins with smooth rims such as treacle tins.

Use your imagination when thinking what to put in: balls go into almost everything, even a ping-pong ball goes into a teapot; bean bags fall into a dirty clothes basket with a most satisfying sound; clothes pegs, plastic hair rollers, large beads, bricks, cotton reels and bobbins (if you haven't got enough ask a local shop if they have any in their workroom that you could have), large buttons, small plastic flowerpots, small tins (with their lids safely sellotaped if they come off easily and are sharp).

Don't throw away anything without looking at it through the eyes of a child who is seeing things for the first time and doesn't yet know about 'rubbish'. Empty lipstick cases can be screwed and unscrewed as well as put into teapots or handbags; empty plastic tubes and bottles that contained cosmetics (remove the smaller screw tops for safety) will offer the added attraction of lingering perfume (decide carefully which containers should be well washed and which can safely and profitably be offered as they are); small boxes go into bigger boxes; silver paper from a bar of chocolate will wrap round a ping-pong ball to give it a new interest; small scrubbed potatoes can be transferred from handbags to tins and back again, and still be eaten afterwards.

The name of the game is simply putting in and taking out.

Some children enjoy being in a play-pen that has a plentiful array of objects attached to the rails by cords of varying length: plastic balls with perforations, plastic shuttlecocks, very small saucepans, plastic colanders and jugs, woolly animals, rag dolls, bean bags, small plastic dustpans. In short, anything that is safe and tie-on-able. It doesn't take long to prepare, and the toddler can explore the variety of shapes and sizes, try swinging those that are on short strings and throwing out those on long ones – but it will be quite a time before he discovers how to pull in the cord to regain the object on the end of it.

In our family I was the only one who enjoyed the play-pen. I used to get in it with all my pins, needles and scissors round me and sew peacefully while the children played round the outside.

Good toy shops offer a wide selection of in-and-out toys. Two particularly popular small ones are the hammer-peg toy and the posting box with different shaped pieces to post through matching holes. You can improvise your own posting box by removing the top of a washing-up liquid container, washing it out thoroughly, cutting it below the neck so that the aperture is big enough to take objects that can't be swallowed, and finding a supply of conkers, butter beans, large beads or shells that will drop through the hole and shake out again. Some containers are transparent, and these offer an extra delight – a child can see the collection grow inside.

Tray jigsaw puzzles are made on the out-and-in principle. The picture is solid and certain objects lift out with a small knob; for example, the cow, horse, farmer and house may be picked out of the picture of a farm. A child may look at the piece in his hand with real attention. He may even name it, or stroke or kiss it if it brings to mind an association with a person or animal that he loves. Or he may not look at the pieces at all but treat them as things to be taken out and given to you, or to be sucked, or thrown or banged together. This is the moment to prevent damage by removing them and showing him how to put them back in their proper place. He may show no interest, in which case put the puzzle away for a few weeks. Or he may suddenly understand what it is all about, and remove the pieces in order to try to replace them himself, with or without success.

Some children learn quite quickly, others are much slower, some try to use force, some give up in frustration. Sometimes it is we who are unreasonable in our expectations. 'That's the place where the horse's nose goes,' we say, forgetting that he may never have seen a horse, or that if he did the large towering animal bore little resemblance to the small piece of coloured plywood in his hand or the hole in the tray. This doesn't mean that we should stop talking naturally and easily as we play with our young children, but that it helps us to be patient if we understand more clearly how much knowledge we possess that is often beyond the toddler's present comprehension.

Another way to play is to 'Put your whole self in, your whole self out'. A large cardboard carton with the lid cut off will hold a small child curled up, and toy firms sell smooth wooden boxes the size of tea-chests, with holes cut in the sides and top through which children can wriggle and crawl. Large dolls' beds, and sturdy wooden dolls' prams will hold a toddler; so will a tin bath or a plastic washing-up bowl or low laundry basket.

There seems to be a universal fascination in curling up into a space that contains us closely, and with toddlers the getting in and getting out is an added joy in its own right.

Up and Down

If you are accustomed to wearing both flat and high-heeled shoes you will know the nature of the difference that high heels make to the way you feel – taller, slimmer, more poised, with a quite marked awareness of looking down on things from a significantly different angle.

It surely isn't surprising that toddlers also delight in being 'up': they love to be picked up just for the pleasure of warm close contact, but once 'up' then watch their delighted faces as they gaze round the unexpected scene. Dads perch them on broad shoulders, and from that vantage-point the excitement can border on fear – it could be the fear of falling, or perhaps it suddenly feels as though they haven't got parents any more when they look up as usual to see them and there isn't anyone up above. The world is so new to children that it is difficult to put ourselves in their place and see with their eyes.

One of the simplest pleasures of early childhood is to mount a single small step, or a box or a thick piece of timber, and then get down again (sometimes with considerable difficulty in learning how to flex the knee of the leg on which the weight rests) in order to get up yet again, and again, and again. The clambering up is an important part of the proceedings, and so is the jumping off, but perhaps the real joy is the standing tall.

It is a good play investment to buy or make strong, simple apparatus that affords children this satisfaction of being 'up' and offers the added bonus of encouraging climbing and balancing skills. There are broad smooth planks that can be raised a few inches off the ground by resting them on 2-inch wooden blocks; wooden variplay stairs; small climbing frames with adjustable platforms that allow toddlers to stand tall whilst holding on to a rail; slides that afford not only the joy of the view from the top but the exhilaration of standing tall then sliding; and hollow building blocks that are strong enough to stand on. All these are very expensive but they have a varied play life for many years to come.

By the time toddlers have discovered climbing apparatus, whether bought or improvised, their skill and confidence match each other remarkably well. They usually know their limitations and will often climb only one step up, then descend again, for quite a long time before venturing further.

But don't leave anything to chance, for one distraught pair of parents suddenly saw their 34-month-old son inspecting the gutter from the top of the housepainter's ladder. He was brought safely down, but some of you will identify your own child as one who can climb with the speed and agility of a monkey whilst having the fearlessness that accompanies the ignorance of dangers not yet experienced. The words 'Be careful, you'll fall' may not arouse caution in him at all, not because he means to be deliberately disobedient but because the only memories he may have of falling may be delightful ones of tripping over on the carpet, grass or sand while you all laugh together, or of being swung safely from ceiling to floor with the teasing words 'You're falling, falling, falling!' while he confidently waits for the critical moment when strong arms sweep him to safety in a hug.

It is only after several unpleasant falls that the warning 'You'll fall' may strike a real warning note, or when the consequences of disobedience are not worth the pleasure of the climb anyway. But eventually the trust built up over a long period, allied to his own experience, inclines him to a trusting obedience.

In the early days of climbing, whether stairs or a climbing frame, a calm reassuring adult needs to be at hand to give the impression of being quite unconcerned whilst being alert to offer a helping hand or words of encouragement. If a caution seems necessary, then 'Slowly' or 'Careful' is more positive and effective than 'Be careful, you'll fall'. The golden rule is not to hurry children.

A toddler trying to climb over a bench or rail for the first time is confronted by hands and feet in the most extraordinary places. If you watch his face as well as his hands and feet as he wobbles and grips and wonders which part of his anatomy to move next, you will see that even changing a hand grip is a major move because he isn't sure where his weight is distributed. And if he is bare-footed you will also see how he uses his big toe as a sensitive feeler for a foothold before the other toes curl and grip.

Once we can disengage our imaginations and fears from our observation of young children climbing, then watching them learn to coordinate and use their limbs effectively is a revelation: so many movements that are automatic for us are genuine problems to be solved by children who have only been in the world for a relatively few months.

We take so much of our own learning for granted that we often deny them valuable experiences because our anticipation of their needs has jumped ahead of their real needs too far and too quickly. We see them struggling to clamber over an obstacle and are apt to say 'Want to get over? Up you come!' as we scoop them up and transfer them to where we thought they wanted to be. The chances are that the other side wasn't the objective at all, it was the getting there that was proving to be such an enthralling and valuable challenge. If we climb up, down, over or through it is almost always as a means to an end: to a toddler the upping, downing, overing and throughing are learning experiences and satisfactions in their own right.

On and Off

The early stages of this game are that you put it on, and the toddler takes it off. You put on his shoes, socks, gloves, and he not only takes them off but stuffs them into his mouth or throws them overboard. The months go by but the game goes on. You put food in front of him, he brushes it off his plate or high-chair tray with one sweep of his hand. You set the table and leave a corner of the tablecloth hanging over the edge, he tugs at it, and not only may everything be broken in a matter of frighteningly noisy seconds but if a cup of hot tea is involved you may have a badly scalded toddler. You put a pile of ironing on a chair ready to take upstairs, he pulls it all over the floor.

There are good days when we are calm enough to see many of the actions spring from sudden impulses, a touching that follows seeing so automatically that there is no intention behind it at all. There are bad days when in our overwrought state it almost seems as though he has deliberately said to himself 'Right! She's spent a couple of hours ironing and I'm going to see how quickly I can knock the pile down and mess everything up so that she has to do it again.'

There are days when action is motivated by curiosity and with careful interest he will take something off somewhere, inspect it, and return it or put it on somewhere else. He may take his socks off, place them carefully on his head, feel and watch them slip down over his nose to fall in his lap, repeat the process with mounting excitement and laughter and invite you to share the joke. There are other days when he is the one who is overwrought, and he runs hither and thither bringing down anything and everything that comes to hand.

Whatever his moods or ours the fact remains that a

great deal of practical onning and offing is needed before he begins to understand what it is all about, so we need to think up different ways of satisfying this very real stage of discovery. The once maddening removal of clothes can lead on to simple dressing up, and another delightful and absorbing stage of play begins. Few toddlers can cope with buttons, press studs, hooks and eyes, or even the complication of sleeves and neck openings at this stage, and they need something that goes on and off in the simplest way.

On one occasion I watched a two-year-old spend half an hour by herself playing with a box of hats which had been given to her after a careful inspection to remove anything that might scratch or constitute danger. There was a large white fur-fabric beret which she stroked, cuddled and rubbed against her cheek before putting it on; it came right down over her nose, and miraculously stayed still while she turned her head from side to side in the warm darkness. She took it off, blinked and looked about her, and then put it on again and blotted out the view. Next she tried a pink and blue knitted tea cosy. She patted the flowers, and explored the holes for the spout and handle with her fingers. A hard riding-hat followed, then an all-enveloping rust velour hat with a large brim; then a beret sewn all over with large shiny buttons; then a lacy wedding hat with a see-through brim, and back to the furry favourite.

Although a mirror at her own height had thoughtfully been provided she didn't once look into it; she was concerned with what she felt like, not looked like, as she put on and took off the hats. She was experiencing them through her senses in a way that we have forgotten: the furry hat felt soft to her fingers and cheek, it hid the room from her in blackness, created warmth inside it, and felt quite heavy on her head; the blocked riding-hat was soft to her fingers, hard to her head, and the peak shut out only the top half of the room in blackness; the tea cosy was squashy-soft in her hands but not furry-soft to her fingers, and when it was on she could pull her hair through the spout and handle holes. She was learning the on-ness of a hat on her head, but also that each 'on' brought with it its own sensations. The 'ons' were different, the 'offs' were the same in this particular play.

Dolls' clothes and covers can be another form of on-and-off play, and some children derive great pleasure from putting a doll in a cot or pram and putting on (and tucking in) layer after layer of sheets, blankets and coverlets. The usual pattern of play is to put all the covers on one at a time, then to pull them off together and start again. It may be that the tucking in is the real satisfaction, and perhaps this in turn is associated by children with the pleasure of being tucked in each night themselves.

I still find this play fascinating to watch, never quite sure whether the joy lies in the mothering or fathering of their 'child' or the practicalities of the bedtime ritual or the simple pleasure of putting things on and taking them off. It is probably all three, though sometimes one factor will be stronger than the others as nature prompts children to play intuitively according to their needs.

Another form of on and off play is that afforded by bricks. Earlier on you probably built towers of bricks, which were knocked down with great gusto, and this led to shared play in which you put one or two bricks on top of each other before handing him the next brick. Toddlers vary greatly in their attitude and ability to build a tower of bricks. Some can slap bricks on top of each other with amazing ease and accuracy, some are very slow and deliberate. Some build for the joy of the knocking down, others blink and draw back near to tears if the tower collapses. Some bang bricks together revelling in the noise in between each placement, some are clearly distressed by the noise rather than the fact that their tower has collapsed.

In spite of these differences there is an almost universal tendency to knock down your tower before building their own; to build up one at a time but to knock down whole-sale, rather than to dismantle one at a time; and then to build more elaborate towers and walls before experimenting with bricks laid end to end over a wide area.

It is worth taking time to introduce your toddler to bricks because once he acquires an interest in them it can lead on to years of rewarding play that takes different forms as the bricks are used in conjunction with little cars, train sets, farm and zoo animals, Lego and construction sets, cranes, wheelbarrows and goodness knows what else. A stout canvas bag of beechwood bricks is an excellent investment, provided you enjoy playing with your child in these early stages so that you can introduce him to their delights. Occasionally build something for your own pleasure, and to give him the idea that there are unlimited play possibilities ahead for him when he is ready.

Over the years I have learned that to suggest bricks as a present for a child who hasn't been played with often leads to the come-back 'You know those bricks? Well, he never plays with them.' Brick play seems particularly to need an adult's encouragement, and then imagination takes over and creativity follows at a later stage. But if your child is one of those who don't show interest in bricks, then don't worry: nothing is right for everybody. Get the bricks out from time to time and play with them yourself. Example is far more stimulating than 'Why don't you play with your bricks?'

All the toy catalogues show a wide range of on-and-off toys in the form of balls, rings or blocks that slip over pegs. These are graded by size, shape and colour so that when the delight of onning and offing is exhausted the toddler can go on to be interested in matching colours and shapes, and later still learn how to grade sizes. For those who show particular aptitude for this there are similar shapes with a differing number of holes in each to correspond to the pegs on the board, but few will be ready for this form of pegboard. There is also a wide variety of simple constructional toys, such as Duplo Lego, Asco bricks, multi-link cubes and others in this family of press-on, pull-off toys.

As you offer fresh toys and experiences to your toddler remember just how new the world and everything in it still is from his point of view. If you are one of those people who hates to be badgered by shop assistants until you have had a chance to look round quietly on your own, then you will appreciate how your child feels. He needs time to investigate and experiment quietly before you intrude on his privacy. Silent concentration is always valuable, and the part you play is to provide the atmosphere of peace and approval in which this can happen, and to share in the play when his concentration slackens and he becomes aware of his suroundings, and you, again.

Pull and Push

The earliest form of pull and push is the grab and pull of 'I want' and the push and shove of 'Take it away', and this spontaneous reaction stays with us all our lives. Sometimes you can see adults draw their plates fractionally towards them after they have been served, and push them fractionally away when they have finished. At crisis point we grab and pull a child quite violently away from danger, or even push him from us with a measure of violence. Since the instinctive pull and push is part of our survival kit, and since play is nature's way of preparing young humans (and animals) for living, it isn't surprising that this form of play lasts so long and takes so many forms.

The first sturdy push-along toys, such as the Baby Walker, are an aid to early walking, combined with a trolley that extends the play possibilities beyond this stage. The next version of this is the small low wooden pram or wagon that is safe for the children to push, or even climb into themselves, whilst being equally satisfactory to transport bricks, shopping or dolls.

Two small push-and-pull toys that combine early walking and play are the Whirligig and Toddle Bell. Each has a rigid handle, the one has a little roundabout with balls that swing out as it revolves, and the other has bells that ring as the wheels turn.

Pull-along toys come in a wide variety, from trucks full of bricks to small trains, cars or boats, dogs and other animals on trolleys and articulated but wheelless caterpillar-type concoctions. These are the sort of presents that we love to give and children love to receive on special occasions, but brought presents should be in addition to, not instead of, home-made improvisations.

An 82-year-old recalling her childhood vividly described her most precious toy and companion. It was her dog Fido, who went everywhere with her and slept in his basket beside her bed. Fido was a knuckle-bone, well boiled and scraped and attached to a length of window-blind cord. Another member of that same generation remembered that she had a little dumb-bell that she trailed after her on a dog lead.

Bones are still available from some butchers' shops and are very easy to keep clean. (But do be careful not to boil Fido, who will be very real to his owner. As you enjoy bathing your child, so he will enjoy bathing his friend.) Bones also bump and clatter along in a most satisfactory way.

Try not to be intimidated by the thought 'What will people think? Will they think we're mean or broke?' Your child should come first, and your child can use his imagination more easily on an object that hasn't been created in a definite likeness. He will also be free from the inhibiting words 'Be careful; you'll hurt it/break it/spoil it' (though he must heed those occasions when you rightly say 'Be careful, Fido is so heavy that he may hurt whatever it is'). You can also explain that you don't want your child to grow up to be the sort of person who values only what can be bought in shops, that you want him to develop the ability to improvise and to experience the satisfaction of do-it-yourself right from the beginning.

Soft versions of pull-along toys are valuable too, and easy to make. One shy little girl became confident once she saw and adopted the long stuffed snake that had been bought to block under-door draughts; she tucked the head under her arm and let the body trail after her. Another small boy found his courage through a 'horse' made out of a stuffed nylon stocking. The foot, with button eyes sewn firmly on it, was the head and the 'body' trailed comfortingly behind.

Clutch or pull-along toys often serve this dual purpose of plaything and comforter: it is as though the child is holding on to something as a substitute for holding your hand, and the feeling of safety is transferred to the chosen object.

In these pre-school years, and often for some time after, children find great difficulty in distinguishing between reality and fantasy and we need to be sensitive to the reality of these inanimate or even invisible companions. A five-foot stuffed snake is highly inconvenient on a bus, but his owner may be happy to leave Snake having a nap stretched full length in your bed; or you can make a baby snake to take out and about so that it can return to tell father or mother snake all the news.

We can't have it both ways: if the love object or safety valve is real enough to turn diffidence to confidence, then it is real enough to be treated with respect.

Another form of pull-and-push play is the propelling and reversing that comes from sitting astride and 'paddling' wheeled toys: cycles with pedals are extremely difficult for young children to manage, and even if you buy a pedalling model the chances are that it will still be paddled. There are some beautiful sturdy wooden trikes, also some metal ones but they are expensive; there are also some large plastic buses, tractors and similar models that are excellent play value since they are relatively cheap, sturdy, easy on paintwork and home furnishings, and offer the joy of movement, the challenge of manipulative skills and the imaginative satisfaction of driving a vehicle.

As the children grow and develop so will their play: instead of being content to pull, push, paddle and reverse just for the physical pleasure and emotional satisfaction these activities afford, they will want to go on to use all these skills as a means to an end rather than as an end in themselves. The doll's pram is no longer just something to push, but the means of taking their 'children' (not dolls to them) for a walk; wagons, trolleys and wheelbarrow are the means of taking things from one place to another, though it may be with no purpose in mind yet other than the satisfaction of adding the skills of loading and unloading to pulling and pushing.

Watch carefully for your own learning, for it can come as something of a shock to realise that toddlers haven't a clue how to turn a corner with a four-wheeled object like a pram. They can steer it in a wide arc but a sharp turn can be a baffling challenge, to be met by much pushing, tugging, even letting go of the handle in order to try a hefty shove in the middle of the side – which can lead to the pram toppling over if it isn't one of the safe low models.

A wheelbarrow is equally baffling. Again and again a child will patiently load up with bricks, grass, cushions or newspapers only to see the whole lot slide off as he lifts the handles. He has no understanding yet about words like tilt or angle, and neither can he recall and reason along the lines of 'Ah! these things are sliding in exactly the same way as I slide down the slide at the park, so that means that the tilted wheelbarrow and the slide have something in common. What is it?'

It is moments like this that help us to see things through the toddler's eyes and limited experience, and then we can offer just as much but no more help than he needs. While he goes on struggling and experimenting he is learning, but he needs to experience success if he is to acquire the habit of struggling to overcome difficulties, so move in to offer help and advice before the frustration goes too far.

One other point – if you have provided something that has been designed to take a load then you also need to give some thought as to what is available to load. If bricks and dolls have outlived their interest for the time being then finding a substitute can often revitalise play. Time is well spent making some small sacks in assorted sizes from strong calico, canvas or workmanlike sale remnants (gay prints don't convey the seriousness of proper work, which is what humping sacks is all about). If needlework isn't for you, then buy a floor cloth, cut it in half, fold each piece in half again and staple the long sides together – being very careful to check that every staple is tightly closed – then turn the sack inside out; or buy a dishwashing cloth made from tubular knitted stockinet material, and cut off the top row of stitching to give you a ready-made sack; or even use a man's sock.

Good sack-fillers are fir cones, small balls of tightly crumpled newspaper, very small logs cut from a broom handle, nuts, small scrubbed potatoes, stones, brussels sprouts, carrots and onions (which can be eaten afterwards), or anything else that comes to mind.

If you spend time together in a greengrocer's shop you will be able to look at the sacks full of vegetables, and this will add to his pleasure in having sacks of his own: he won't be 'playing with food', he will be playing the sort of play through which he will eventually come to understand that some bulky things are light in weight, some small packages are heavy, some stack easily, some don't, that some food comes from shops, and that some of it gets to the shops in sacks even though some get to freezers in plastic packs.

In the early stages of a new form of play the less we say the better, for so often our words stifle the very play that we are trying to encourage. Our job is to be imaginative enough to keep an eye open for new ways of offering variations for these basic 'doings' of toddlers, and to see that they are readily available and that he knows he has our permission and approval to use them.

Once the sacks are made the first suggestions can come from him. Say 'What shall we put in this one?' and try to agree with his suggestions as often as possible lest he comes to feel that he is incapable of having good ideas. It is when he runs out of ideas that we can say 'I wonder if we could find some small brussels sprouts?' and the looking together for the right sort to go in a small sack can be a pleasure bonus.

Needless to say, the making of sacks and the slow browsing through a large bag of sprouts together is no occupation for a busy morning. These are the sort of things to do when the morning chores are over and the evening ones haven't yet begun, or when it is 'just one of those days' and you know that in the long run it will pay hands down to give your toddler your undivided attention – especially in a form that may open up new play possibilities for him, and peace and quiet for both of you.

Hide and Seek

The game begins very early with peep-bo! and continues with variations for the rest of our lives, and if we can identify some of the ways in which we still play it then it becomes easier to understand our children's satisfaction in hiding and seeking.

We hide presents in the pleasurable anticipation of producing them on the right day. If we hide sweets we do it with deliberation so that they don't offer constant temptation. We may sometimes hide a new purchase with guilt or anxiety and wait for a tactful moment to bring it out. We may cheerfully, shamefully or as a matter of course hide things under cushions or beds for a quick tidy up. If our childhood memories or more recent experiences are too painful we may still feel tempted to hide the evidence of breakage, damage or waste for fear of the consequences. We may also hide our feelings for fear of other people's reactions.

Hiding is accompanied by a wide range of emotions, some of them very unpleasant, but finding is mostly associated with pleasant emotions.

We have all had the experience of mislaying something and searching, worrying and puzzling sometimes for days until in a joyful flash we remember where we left or even hid it. We lose our way walking or driving and grow increasingly uneasy until suddenly we find a landmark and relief floods through us. We make an effort to be friendly with someone who seems cold or antagonistic, and find the warm and likeable person hiding behind the barriers that were erected through shyness or anxiety.

Conversely, we are sometimes drawn to someone who has all the qualities we like, or need at the time, only to find something destructive hidden beneath the surface, and then the 'finding' is a shock. And as we seek, find and

90

sometimes lose people, so they seek, find, and sometimes lose us because we weren't quite what they thought we were either.

We need to relive all these memories as we watch our children play for although their early joys of hide and seek are the simple magic of 'Now it's here! Now it's not!' these first games and our reactions to them are part of the whole growing-up process. Watch a toddler playing with sand and you will almost certainly see him hide shells, the spade and sand moulds, his feet and small toys. If he is digging in the garden then stones, daisies, the dog's bone, a clothes peg, a leaf will be busily hidden in order to be rediscovered. If it is dough he will hide sultanas, a teaspoon, the pastry cutters or his fingers in the lump.

The practical relevance of recalling our own experience is that in moments such as these we can glance at his face as well as his hands, and if his expression is one of blissful satisfaction we can often allow the play to continue without interruption. If we look only at his hands we are apt to compare what he is doing with our own intentions for him, and then we say 'What have you done to your nice gingerbread man? You've spoilt him!' The very fact that the gingerbread man is 'spoilt' indicates that that particular game played with you is now over, and he has reverted to hide and seek or yet another form of play on his own. Let him play it out if you possibly can for it is valuable in its own right, and you can still cook the end product when the play is over.

Don't imagine for a moment that I am saying that you must always let children do what they want to do: that would make life quite impossible for everyone. The suggestion is only that you have second thoughts before jumping in with 'No, don't' too often. Naturally the entire contents of the peg bag can't be buried in mud, but if only one peg is involved there are several lines of thinking that can be followed before you take action:

1   You can rescue your peg, which may be your instinctive reaction.

2   You may decide to give him that particular peg at the end of his play with it, saying 'Would you like to keep that special peg to play with another day?'

3   You may decide that the period of peacefulness is valuable for both of you, even if the peg is lost altogether.

4   You may resolve to rescue the peg and wash it yourself after the play has finished.

5   You may accept that the peg, especially if it is made of wood, won't be fit for clothes again but will still be serviceable for dusters or floorcloths.

6   You may plan ahead for another peaceful period of play when you give him a bowl of soapy water and a nailbrush so that he can wash both the peg and his hands afterwards.

At this particular moment you may be so wound up that you don't know whether to laugh, cry or scream at the idea of stopping to think out all these alternatives – I remember the feeling only too well. But I also remember just such a mother on a playgroup course saying:

'I started playing a game with myself to see if I could get through an hour without saying "No, don't", and at first I couldn't. I couldn't think what to say instead. And then I found that sometimes while I was still thinking she'd stop doing it anyway. And other times as I was looking and trying to think I suddenly saw that what she was doing wasn't really doing any harm anyway. After that it got easier not to be so quick off the mark and it made life a lot easier for both of us, and then I didn't feel so bad when I was jolly well determined that she wasn't going to do some of the things she wanted to do.'

At this stage both you and your toddler are probably afraid of losing each other quite literally and it may help you to be patient with the endless hide and seek games if you realise that they are playing their part in preparing him to cope more easily with the fear of being lost. Most of us can remember the childhood panic of being lost temporarily in the crowds on a beach or in a shop, and if we see such a child it is instinctive to go down to his level and to say confidently 'Are Mummy and Daddy lost? It's all right, we can soon find them.'

A child who has a rich play experience of hiding and seeking and losing and finding behind him is likely to be easier to comfort than one without such a preparation through play. The playing will have given him confidence that losing and finding almost always go together and his repeated experiences go some way towards making his fear more manageable.

An enjoyable version of hide and seek play is the glad-bag: it can be a large knitting bag, or a carrier bag, or a handbag or holdall that snaps or zips shut to add to the 'lostness'. You can sit comfortably with the bag on your lap, indoors, in the garden if you have one, in the park or on the beach, and your toddler can hunt for treasures to hide in the bag. Each act of hiding can be a ceremony of opening wide and shutting tight, to be reversed eventually when he is invited to thrust his hand in to see what he can find. Although he found and put everything in, and therefore in theory he knows exactly what is inside, you may find that he is afraid to plunge his hand into a dark hiding place. If this is so respect his feelings and understand that the impact of the dark trap confronting him is so strong that it blots out the visual memory of what is inside. Either open the bag wide or bring the objects out yourself in the spirit of seek and find.

Later on he will be able to thrust his hand into the bag and guess by feel alone which object his hand has closed round. Later still you can hide assorted objects for him to identify by feel, and you will be reminded again how difficult it is for children to remember things we take for granted. He may be familiar with hair rollers, key rings, bananas and tins of sardines, but as he doesn't associate them together in one place it may be quite difficult to feel, and then to visualise what he is feeling and recall where he usually is when he feels that particular object.

Another form of the game is hiding oneself. This usually begins along the lines of 'Let's surprise Daddy and hide behind the curtains', but toddlers can't usually wait to be found, and rush out saying 'I was hiding!' If you hide and call out 'Ready!' or 'Find me!' you may discover that he doesn't seem able to locate you by the direction from which your voice comes. If you last hid behind the armchair, then that is where he is likely to look first. If you are not where you were last time, then he is likely to look in the other places where he has found you on other occasions. At this stage distress can set in quite quickly if you are too well hidden, and impatience to be found will manifest itself equally quickly if he is the one hiding and you try to prolong his suspense.

This is a valuable game to play for fun, as long as you remember that the real fear of losing you, or being left alone by you, are very near the surface.

Do and Undo

Needless to say toddlers are much better at undoing than doing, but that is true of all of us.

I remember with gratitude a period when our toddler was fascinated by unlacing shoes. Whenever one or both of us needed a quiet uninterrupted half-hour all I had to do was to assemble on the kitchen floor every pair of lace-up shoes that my husband and I possessed – tennis and gym shoes, cricket and football boots, walking and gardening shoes. Slowly and methodically our son removed every lace, which took a long time because some of them were very long and presented quite a problem and others had bent tags which also slowed things down nicely. He would then put small shoes inside big shoes and play trains along the floor with the biggest shoes. When it came to the relacing my husband and I tackled it together and felt that it was well worth the small expenditure of time and effort.

Repetition is soothing to most children, and they enjoy a slow 'doing', to be followed by a rapid undoing. But their ability to use their hands varies greatly so it will be a matter of trial and error to find the activity that your particular child finds absorbing.

Some toddlers will enjoy doing a simple jigsaw puzzle, and in addition to the small picture trays with the objects that lift out by means of a knob you may like to try the giant variety made for physically and mentally handicapped children but much enjoyed by all children. In these, the pieces rise above the background and are easy to lift out and replace.

Threading is very difficult for some children but others pick it up quite quickly. Toy catalogues offer coloured cotton reels and large wooden beads, and the beads for handicapped children are larger still in five different shapes and with a stiffened end on the cord for easy threading.

Screw rods come in two types, those with identical plastic nuts and those with nuts in different shapes (which make the unscrewing slower than with the identical nuts, which children soon learn to unscrew two or three at a time by a quick stroke with the palm of the hand). For those with nimble fingers there is a small wooden play-bench fitted together with nuts, bolts, screws and pegs.

Bearing in mind children's love of repetition, it is easy to see how it comes about that once they have found a 'doing' job that fascinates them they will carry on as long as possible. Most of us have suffered from a toddler who discovered the delight of snapping off tulip heads, poking holes in upholstered chairs with a knitting needle, pulling cherries off a trifle.

Being human, we are exasperated, but if we thought a bit we might find similar activities that would be harmless. It doesn't have to be tulip heads. Pea pods snap in the same satisfactory way, and seed beans can be broken out of their pods. Decorations could be put on to a trifle or cake – or mud-pie – instead of being taken off. Holes can be poked into left-over pieces of pastry, either with a finger or with a blunt wooden skewer or spoon handle.

Every time you catch your toddler doing something that he shouldn't do, ask yourself if you could find something that he could do.

Look and Show

One of the delights of the toddler stage is that everything is still so new that there are endless opportunities to hold out something that he is seeing for the first time, saying 'Look!', and then to watch the wonder, surprise, doubt, interest or amusement on his face, followed almost always by the stretching out of his hands to touch. But there are some days when he is already looking at and exploring something that he has discovered for himself, and in our tiredness and frustration we say sharply 'Look out . . . look what you're doing . . . look where you're going', or even illogically 'Why don't you *look*?'

When we say 'Look what you're doing!' what we probably mean is 'I can see that you are looking intently at every single scarlet petal as you pull it off the tulips, but can't you see what you are doing to my feelings?' He can't, of course, until we teach him, and this sort of teaching grows easier as we learn to distinguish more clearly between what *he* sees and feels, and what *we* see and feel as we behold him seeing and feeling.

Our three-year-old taught me this lesson. He used to come with me each morning to hang out the baby's nappies. He carried the peg bag and handed the pegs to me one at a time, or we would change over (if I was calm and patient that morning) and he would hand me the nappies – only often he would pick up one and drag the next one over the edge of the basket on to the path, hence the need to be feeling cheerful enough to say 'Never mind, we'll wash that one again.'

One day I looked out of the kitchen window and saw him sitting in the middle of the path with his back to me, intent upon something that I couldn't see. Minutes later he was still there, and I glanced at my watch to see how long this intense concentration would last. After nine minutes I was priding myself on what an intelligent child we had – at fifteen minutes I was suddenly panic-stricken, suppose he was systematically eating poison berries? (In moments like this your emotion is so strong that it doesn't give your intelligence a chance to say 'What poison berries? You know perfectly well that you eradicated every single one from the garden before the children were even born!')

I went down the garden path with forced calm, and stood watching him for quite a time before he even saw me. He was seeing – really seeing – a clothes peg for the first time. He had worked out how it opened and shut, but he couldn't make it clip on. Every now and then he turned it upside down and slipped the open end astride the top of his dungarees, where the pressure of his jersey held it precariously in position. It was almost as though he was saying to himself, 'I really must feel a bit of success to encourage me to go on trying – I know it's not right, but at least it is attached in a sort of a way to my clothes.'

He slipped the open end over the cuffs of his jersey and, quite unsuccessfully, on to his trouser leg hems; he tried to force various bits of clothing between the shut 'teeth'; he tried to poke his finger and a shoe lace through the hole where the clothes line would normally be; he abandoned the clothes part of the problem and with great satisfaction, and two hands, pressed the open ends together to open the 'mouth'. He tried to advance the open 'mouth' towards his trouser leg, but every time he got the timing wrong, and he snapped the spring before the material was safely in the 'mouth'.

Suddenly his concentration wavered and he looked as though he was either about to burst into tears or throw the peg from him in exasperation. He saw me at that point, and we sat on the path together, and he fixed the peg triumphantly on the taut hem of my dress which I advanced towards his open-mouthed peg.

My respect for him was immense, and I was glad

he had reminded me yet again that my everyday tasks done without hesitation were, to him, not only mysteries but physically taxing feats of endurance. We fixed him up a nice taut washing-line round the legs of the kitchen table, and his favourite occupation for days was returning to the table at intervals to fix a few more pegs securely on the line.

All too often we interrupt a child who has begun to look with more than his eyes. He may be looking with problem-solving intelligence to try to make sense of what he sees, as with the clothes pegs, or he may be looking with suspicion, weighing up the pros and cons in an intuitive sort of way, as he surveys a large strange animal whose head comes up to his chest and listens to a voice say 'Pat the doggie, he won't hurt you.'

There is also the look of open-ended curiosity – no fear, no suspicion, no burning urge to explore, just a nice interested 'What's that then?' Men digging up a road, a police car with the blue light flashing, a large red bus, a painter's ladder against a wall, a man carrying a dust-bin, a mechanical road sweeper, a little old person bent almost double and shuffling along, a dog barking behind a gate. A lovely procession of things viewed from the safety of a pushchair or a walk holding hands.

Sometimes real interest is sparked, and he really does want to stand and stare. Do let him if you possibly can for it will pay off handsomely for both of you. If he was really intrigued he will ask you next day if he can go and have another look, and another and another. Try to allow time for this for by the time he has watched the petrol pump attendant with ever-growing attention for several days you may well find that he is happy and busy playing at petrol pump men for several more days.

This sort of imitative play is the very stuff of childhood and is valuable beyond price. But you will have to watch with eyes as sharp as his, for if you don't he is likely to go home, find a piece of rope, tie it on to the water-butt tap, turn the tap full on, and stand holding the other end of the rope close to the back of his lorry – and you will shout 'Turn that tap off! Look what you're doing! Look at all that water!'

If you have watched the petrol pump attendant as closely as he has you will know exactly what he is doing, as surely as you will also know exactly why he can't do it. Your understanding will enable you to bridge the gap so that the flood of water ceases but the play can go on. You will probably turn the water off with all speed explaining that it is needed to water the plants, but you may also go on to offer to fix his rope, or a piece of hose-pipe, to another petrol pump post.

Children have marvellous imaginations, and if you go with them rather than against them you can follow up your various joint lookings by helping him to find a trouble-free way of reproducing what he wants to imitate. This sort of play is long-lasting and satisfying for both of you, and costs nothing but your ability to organise your walks in such a way that you allow for time to stand and stare occasionally.

But a word of warning: if you grow too enthusiastic and start saying things like 'Would you like to play that when we get back? I could find you a — and we could make a — and we'll ask Daddy for his —', then you'll turn him off altogether – and what's more he'll do what we do when other people start making our plans for us, he'll go all quiet and flat or get irritable and scratchy because everything's been spoilt.

One of the most precious forms of looking is the one we kill most often: it is the look of pure wonder, when the degree and nature of the surprise literally stops him in his tracks and he is held transfixed in one of those moments that knows no equal at any age. It may be his first sight of the sea in all its shimmering vastness, or a spider spinning a web under the kitchen sink, or waking up to a snow-covered world for the first time, or seeing a puddle in the gutter that shines with all the colours that he has ever seen. These are moments to be shared in silence for as long as the spell holds; he needs time to take in what he is seeing and experiencing through all his senses, and time just to be aware of the moment itself. Can you remember the feeling of awareness as you woke for the first time to a room filled with the strange lightness and brightness of snow? If you can, then the moment will come back to you as you watch your child half feel, half think 'What is it? Something strange. Nice? Odd! Different! Exciting!' It is a moment to be savoured in silence and come through slowly.

Let your child remind you of your own childhood, for the more memories come back to you the more you will identify with your child and the easier it becomes to understand and enjoy him.

Another delightful and valuable way of looking together is to share books. Children love the feeling that they have your undivided attention, the close proximity and comfort of sitting on your lap, the atmosphere of peaceful enjoyment, and the books themselves. Sometimes they like you to turn the pages over slowly and silently, content just to look. Sometimes they like you to talk about the pictures quietly, asking questions that don't need an answer – 'There's a cat, she's fast asleep, isn't she?' Sometimes they like the commentary to be bright and lively, sometimes they want to be asked questions that they can answer, and sometimes they want an illustrated story to be read again and again and again until they know it so well that they can correct the mistake of a single misplaced word.

One father told me that he and his son knew *The Tale of Peter Rabbit* by heart, and one day he found the same edition with a German text so he took it home and when story-time arrived he produced the new book and read it from cover to cover in German. His child didn't appear to notice the difference!

Fill and Empty

You don't need anyone to tell you that the emptying stage comes first. The cornflakes are emptied into the washing machine, the salt into the sugar, the milk into the potted geranium, the button-box on to the floor.

Sometimes it is a case of mistaken identity – the corn-flake and Persil packets are similar in size and shape. Sometimes we confuse children, as I did when I used a milk jug to water the plants and top up the vases. Sometimes it just seems to be an irresistible urge, and probably many of us can remember tipping the salt into the sugar with immense satisfaction and pleasure in the act just for its own sake, and with no thought at all as to the consequences. (If you have never tasted salt and sugar in tea how can you know how foul it is?) The fact that toddlers truly don't understand what they are doing on some occasions often escapes our notice or if we do understand it still doesn't always help us to be patient.

We know that if water is spilt on the kitchen lino tiles that have only just been stuck down it may harm them (even if it wouldn't we would still *feel* anxious in the early days after spending so much time and money on the job). Our toddler knows nothing of all this. He may be playing quite happily and innocently with a bowl of water at the sink, and a jug, and a large funnel. He may discover that water poured into a funnel does something funny, and much more exciting than if you pour it into another jug. In delight, and with that same old longing to share his pleasure with you, he may say 'Look' and before you can draw breath he has turned from the sink with the jug in one hand, the funnel in the other, and is pouring the water through and on to the floor.

No one in their right senses would suggest that you just stand there smiling and saying 'Lovely! Do it again' but, if there is a flash in which you really do understand that he is only able to take in the picture of the water pouring into the funnel and out at the bottom, then you will also understand that he isn't yet aware of where the water goes after it leaves his delighted gaze at the bottom of the funnel.

You will still sprint to block the funnel with your hand as you direct it back over the sink, but you may be able to say simultaneously 'It's all right' as you realise in that split second how totally bewildered he must feel. There he was, having a lovely time, and being kind enough to let you in on his lovely time, and you went and shouted and nearly knocked him flying!

We have to accept the fact that he's got gallons and gallons of pour-out-ability inside him that needs to be released during the next few years, and nature will see to it that he *does* go through this vital stage. So all we can do is to devise ways of letting him fill and empty that will be pleasurable and valuable to him, and doubly pleasurable and valuable to you, first because you are encouraging him to do what he has to do if he is going to play in the way that lays down the foundations for all later learning, and secondly because a peacefully employed child is so much easier to live with.

Once you begin to think about it you will find many ways to provide filling and pouring play that need cause no anxiety. Silver sand is a delight to the touch, and a seven-pound bag in a small plastic washing-up bowl will give soothing pleasure on countless occasions. Put the bowl on the floor in the middle of a candlewick bedspread, so that spilt sand won't spread all over everywhere, or else use a dust sheet or an old rug or blanket. At first, just offer the sand alone so that your toddler is not denied the first simple experience of plunging his hands into it, scooping it up, letting it trickle through his fingers and generally feeling the full range of sensations that this offers. Then add something like a small plastic egg-cup, a cream carton and a yogurt pot. When this play grows stale take these things out and offer one or two small plastic flowerpots with slits in the bottom, and watch him discover how to put one hand underneath to catch the steady streams of sand that emerge. Have a very small metal teapot handy, and offer it with an egg cup, jug or yogurt carton so that it can be filled by hand or with one of the other containers. Offer a few things at a time rather than everything at once or the sand will disappear under a mountain of objects, and just be quietly at hand to keep the sand confined to the floor covering until the habit of confining play to this area is established.

A few small objects nearby will offer a different form of play, and some children will combine pouring and tipping with hide and seek if conkers, fir cones or shells are available.

When the dry sand has lost its appeal add water to it until it is damp enough for a sand pie to be turned out of a cream carton or flower pot. If he wants it dry again it will dry overnight in shallow trays in the airing cupboard, or spread thinly over the floor covering. Another variation is to offer two washing-up bowls, or one bowl and a large meat tin, for there seems to be a particular satisfaction in taking something out of one place and transferring it to another.

Water is perhaps the greatest delight of all, but only you know whether or not you feel you can cope with it set up in the same way as the dry sand only with a large piece of plastic sheeting or a groundsheet put down in place of the candlewick bedspread. If you are not ready to cope with this, then the washing-up bowl in the sink will allow for all the same filling and emptying, plus washing up plastic cups and saucers or blowing bubbles. One point to watch is the standing accommodation: a stool or chair will make the play possible, but be prepared for the fact that children become so engrossed in what they are doing that they can forget where they are, and they will need to have their attention drawn to the fact that they must get down before moving away.

In the summertime it is possible for those with gardens to have paddling pools, tin baths, or washing-up bowls of water on the grass. But don't leave the children unattended for a single minute – drowning or death from the shock can happen so quickly and a child doesn't even have to be fully immersed to drown. The less clothing the better, for the great joy is the caress of water on the skin.

Don't be in too much of a hurry to do all the work for your busy active toddler, for your work is his play. Why carry several heavy buckets of water out to the bath or pool yourself when this denies him the satisfaction of running to you with a small empty pail, waiting for it to be filled, and then staggering importantly and awkwardly off to enjoy the splash as it is delivered at the other end? The pleasure lies not only in the emptying and filling but in taking the water from one place to another.

Once you understand the nature of the entertainment, then there is an endless variety of ways to meet it – toddlers don't tire of an activity itself so much as the immediate form it takes.

Noise-making and Listening

There was a time when we felt sure our children would go down the aisle to be married making brrum-brrum or bang-bang noises, but after giving years and years of deep satisfaction and pleasure both noises eventually died a natural death.

If you try out the noise for yourself you will begin to see that it isn't just an 'I'm a car' noise, it really is very satisfying. You can feel the vibration behind your cheeks, the flutter of your tongue behind your teeth, the tingling of your lips, and the feeling of being airborne on the waves of noise when they are loud, and soothed and satisfied when they are soft. Unlike words in these early years, sounds can burst forth spontaneously to convey feelings and since there is clearly great enjoyment in this sort of sound-making toddlers should be helped to extend the pleasure.

It is doubly worth singing nursery rhymes and jingles and doing finger games, partly for their own sake as a child's heritage but also to introduce your child to forms of pleasure in sounds that he can make for himself. Children find it very difficult to sing in tune, but the desire is there to break out of silence or the speaking voice into another form of voice, and singing seems to give no less pleasure for being out of tune in these early attempts. Children often have a remarkable ability to imitate sounds, or to repeat words or phrases that give pleasure. Months after Christmas children can be quietly chanting, or murmuring or shouting 'Jingle bells, jingle bells, jingle bells', and when a particular song was at the height of its popularity some very young children learned to say 'supercallifragilisticexpialidotious' with immense enjoyment.

Noises that come from within the toddler are one

106

pleasure, but another is noises that he can make between himself and an object. He can run a stick along railings, and then a metal cooking spoon along those same railings, and then a plastic spoon, and the sound is quite different each time. He can bang a saucepan with its lid (which you won't be able to stand for many seconds); but find a different sound by banging it with a wooden spoon, or a spoon with a folded duster securely tied over it.

You will soon discover that making noise pleases him in two different ways – first as a physical need to bash something hard, with the satisfaction that comes from aggression accompanied by a loud noise; secondly, as a constant source of interest in that almost everything he touches has a different sound, and that this varies according not only to the strength he uses but to what he uses as the striker. Noises in the first category can be catered for by such toys as the peg-hammer toy, where ten stout wooden pegs can be bashed through their holes with a stout wooden hammer, and then the toy can be turned upside down and they can be bashed back again. This is a workmanlike and legitimate way to make a most satisfactory noise.

A selection of drums can be improvised or bought, but do steer clear of the tin drums, the noise is penetrating and has no musical quality at all. A very pleasing sound can be obtained from a Tupperware-type pudding basin with its own tightly fitting lid. This can be tapped with the fingers or slapped by the flat of the hand, or banged with the fist or a small wooden spoon. It is also a good size and shape to tuck under a child's arm as he sits or walks about banging – you may be surprised how naturally some children walk and bang in rhythm.

Jingle bells, Indian bells, rattles and home-made shakers all allow him to make noises, which is not the same thing as making a noise (though that goes on being necessary too).

Whether or not children learn to listen is up to us. They

107

will give up and turn a deaf ear if we continually nag or scold, or if we laugh at behaviour one day for which they are slapped on another, or if we bore them, or if we invade their private quiet moments, or if our talking is like incessant background music, or if we never talk to them at all. But, if toddlers and parents enjoy each other, then they will want to listen to each other, and if they listen to each other then they will enjoy listening to other sounds together.

There are many sounds that need to be recognised and interpreted, for if children don't learn to 'read' sounds as well as they are already learning to 'read' their parents' feelings and moods, then they won't be sufficiently interested and alert to 'read' pictures, practical situations (if the milk is spilt we need a cloth to mop it up), weather, tones of voice, and finally words.

Can your toddlers recognise the sound of an aeroplane, a car, a train, a dog, a saucepan boiling over, your footsteps on the stairs, different people's footsteps on the stairs, the voices of close relations and friends even before the people appear, letters flopping on to the mat, the kettle boiling, a tap running, a clock ticking? When you can hear a sound that he doesn't appear to have registered, catch his eye and say 'Listen! What can you hear?' and see just how many sounds he can recognise.

But remember, too, the need your child has to listen to silence peacefully. Later he may well go through the adolescent stage of wanting every light on all day, and loud music to accompany him wherever he goes, but if he has once learned to be comfortable with silence he can come back to valuing it later on.

A group of mothers were discussing this one day in a deeply deprived area. One mother said: 'I'm scared to death of silence, I came from a huge family and never remember being either alone or quiet, and when my husband's at work and the kids are at school I nearly go mad. I turn the radio up loud and take it from room to room with me, but I could never ever spend a night alone, not even with the lights and radio full on.'

A gran said: 'I have my two grandsons to bring up and I'm too old for all their capers and I get tired . . . I get tired in myself if you know what I mean . . . but as long as I can have our few rooms to myself for a time each day I'm all right. When the place is quiet and empty I can sort of feel myself expand and I'm peaceful.'

Only the first speaker in the group feared silence and aloneness, the rest craved it and several agreed that the only place they could find it was to lock themselves in the loo. Some recognised this same need in their children, especially some, to be able to crawl away and hide under a bed for a while if that was the only place where they could be alone. One father of a four-year-old found his son hiding quietly and said 'What are you doing?'. The child replied 'Thinking.' The father said 'What are you thinking?' and the child replied 'I don't know yet, I haven't finished.'

At every age we must recognise and respect children's need for peace and privacy.

Touch and Feel

Perhaps the heading for this section should be 'Touch and Don't Touch' since the refrain that runs through the days tends to be 'Don't touch, put it down . . . don't touch, it's hot . . . don't touch, he might bite . . . don't touch, it's dirty . . . don't touch, the lady will be cross . . . don't touch, you'll hurt it . . . *Don't touch!*'

Shopping can be exhausting. We need all our concentration to buy wisely, but we have to keep an eye on our toddler, handbag, shopping bags, pushchair or trolley (and sometimes a baby as well) and often there is a background anxiety lest our offspring incurs the disapproval of shop assistants or shoppers.

We pick up a tin, because actually holding it helps us to think. 'Big tins are usually more economical than small ones. On the other hand the big one will be too much for one meal and what could we have tomorrow to use it up?' We dither, and still firmly holding the tin say sharply 'Don't touch!' as our toddler squats to examine the small tins on the bottom shelf.

We constantly touch, and tell our toddler not to. *Children must touch*, or we shall stop their learning before they even start. We take our own knowledge so much for granted that we can no longer even imagine the thousands of times we must have touched before we could record and recall the physical and emotional memories that give real meaning to such words as smooth, rough, sticky, prickly, sharp, blunt, edge, side, corner, square, round, wet, dry, damp, soaking. This list could go on indefinitely and it hasn't even included the animal, vegetable, mineral categories.

Neither has it taken into account the many different contexts in which children may hear a single word: light the fire, it's quite light to carry, a light colour, alight here for . . ., light-hearted, lightweight, light-fingered, and light as opposed to darkness. A further complication for children is that they may have very different emotional memories for a single word: a cold ice-cream is lovely, being cold in bed is miserable, having a cold is worse. Only when we understand and sympathise with the immensity of the task that lies before each child will we begin to understand that touching and feeling is vital as a means of knowing.

If you have any photographs of yourself as a child look them out and study them carefully. With any luck you may be able to remember the occasions well enough to recapture how you felt as you dug in the sand, stood primly in your best clothes, picked daisies on the lawn or sat shelling peas on the door step. If you remember the happiness and satisfaction of 'doing' and 'being' it is easier to put yourself in your child's place and to watch with new eyes.

One meticulously neat and tidy mother saw a film of her immaculate little daughter playing with dough in her playgroup. She watched the ceaselessly moving hands stroke and slap, pummel and punch, twist and squeeze, poke and mould, whilst her lips parted, closed, pursed and smiled and her tongue even came out as she concentrated particularly hard. At the end of the short film the mother was in tears and said 'I've had her for four years and this is the first time I've ever really seen her.'

Begin to think about the different categories of 'feeling' that are part of a toddler's daily experience, skin-feel, shape-feel, weight-feel, water-feel, weather-feel. All this feeling is accompanied by a range of emotional feelings that are, in turn, largely affected by our own attitude of approval or disapproval.

Skin-feel

Gather together a collection of materials that will offer your toddler as many different 'feels' as possible, but first try a simple experiment.

Find a sheet of smooth tissue paper and imagine that you don't even know that it is 'paper', or 'white', or that it is called 'tissue'. You have to learn about it from the beginning, but without the ability or the vocabulary to make a running commentary on what you are doing and learning. It is easy to pick up although it is large. It's light and bright and a bit dazzling. If you pick it up and wave it about it moves in a most peculiar way, not in the least like waving a handkerchief. It feels funny in the palms of your hands, sort of soft, yet not the sort of soft you want to rub against your top lip. You can't throw it away, it seems to want to stay with you – but if it's squashed small it will throw away. You can pull it apart and after a while you can't find your nice big piece any more, it's gone, and all you've got instead is a lot of little ones. They don't taste of anything much, but suddenly there is a soggy wet thing in your mouth and someone is hastily putting a large finger in to fish it out, and there's a lot of dribble, and there's something on her finger – but goodness knows what – and where's the original white stuff?

As a baby your toddler may have gone through all these stages of play (for that is what it is) several times, but that doesn't mean that he knows all about it as we do. You may think he has finished playing with tissue paper, especially as he throws it away when he tries to unwrap a parcel. On his first Christmas he didn't know the difference between paper and present. They were both new and interesting but the chances are that the paper was much easier to handle and was therefore preferred to the present. One or two years later he knows about presents and is in a hurry to get to them so he discards the paper.

It is worth offering him another chance to give tissue paper a further investigation but you will need to introduce it in such a way that it catches his attention anew. Interest can often be sparked by holding a whole new sheet aloft like an open umbrella and saying 'Watch!' as you let it go. Then watch his face as he watches the paper sail, swoop or flap its way down to the ground according to the degree of draught. If he is not interested, leave it alone. If he is intrigued, then be careful not to break into his private world of curiosity, wonder and exploration. Just sit quietly watching, ready to be included when his concentration slackens, and as you watch you will begin to see through your child's eyes, and imagination and insight will guide you to making a collection of other materials.

Velvets are lovely to touch, and come in rich jewel colours – to delight his eyes as well as his fingers, which are discovering the different sensations of stroking with and against the pile. Loosely woven curtain nets can be seen through, and some have a lacy pattern that offers finger-poking holes. Brocades look as though they are going to be good to touch, but then you can see both hands and face react to the strange metallic feel of the interwoven threads. Chamois leather has a softness all its own; so does wide double satin ribbon. Fluted tea-cosies have a satisfactory squashiness, so do small woolly balls.

Plastics can be wet-look, crinkly, shiny, dull, transparent, coloured on one side and dull on the other. Leather has its own distinctive smell and taste. (Can you remember chewing the leather strap of your pram harness?) Gloves with their assortment of fingers do unexpected things on small hands – fur fabric-backed or lined gloves, big driving gauntlets, soft fabric gloves, mittens. A pink rubber glove with holes in the finger tips inspired a farm child to hold it under the tap with one hand while she 'milked her cow' with the other.

Artificial flowers, braces, a strand of Christmas tinsel, cellophane and foil sweet papers, all catch the eye and invite handling. Sometimes toddlers like one single thing to explore without distraction, but at other times they like the temptation and generosity of a large assortment in which to dig and delve. So often we say 'Careful . . . one at a time' that it is as good for us as it is for our children to say occasionally 'There!' as we give liberally.

Shape-feel

All objects have skin-feel, but this collection is intended to be felt in a rather different way: it isn't only the touch against the skin but the exploration of the shapes with the fingers bending and flexing as the muscles enable the whole hand to explore in three dimensions.

Hair curlers come in all shapes and sizes and, although some with bristles and wires might be unsuitable, many are in plastic lattice-work with ridges of small spines not big enough to hurt, but fascinating to feel. We know that they are hollow cylinders with perforations and spines, but the toddler only knows that they are different whichever way you look at them or touch them and it may be a long time before he discovers that a small one will slip inside a larger one. Unless, that is, you give him a dozen in assorted sizes and colours all at once, with nothing else to distract him.

Try wooden spoons and plastic spatulas, tea or coffee strainers, simple egg whisks and shoe trees. They all have their differences and surprises.

Good toy shops sell small playthings to delight the eyes and hands, beautiful carved wooden animals, attractive plastic farm and zoo animals, a bag of one hundred attractive little figures in ten different colours and shapes, translucent shapes that fit together, mosaics, beads. There are sets of plastic men, or elephants, that can be explored on their own or fitted together; the fingermajig, a strong

plastic ball with protruding buttons that can be pushed-
in-here only to send another pushed-out-there; also the
'bendy' animals and figures that can be manipulated by
small hands.

Nests of Russian dolls have a wide appeal, the biggest
one taking apart to reveal another, and another, and
another, until the tiniest one has been discovered. They
come in sets of from three to thirty, but the very smallest
figures could easily be swallowed and are best removed
for a few years.

Some toddlers may not have wanted the traditional
rattles, shakers, bangers and soft toys which you thoughtfully provided in the early months, but later on they may
enjoy going back to make good these missed play stages
so it is worth keeping some of these earliest toys available
for a rainy day.

Weight-feel

Skin-feel and shape-feel will still be there but now there
is an extra sensation as the toddler's muscles not only bend
and flex but begin to register the variations between light
and heavy. He will be doing this all day and every day
anyway as he fetches and carries, picks up and puts down.
But you can gather together a collection of objects that
allow him to experience several different weight-sensa-
tions one after the other as he picks things up at random.

Golf balls and ping-pong balls, a cricket ball (don't
leave him alone with this!) and a rubber ball, a balloon
and a beach ball – just let him play with them all quite
naturally for he will need a great deal of repeated experience before he knows in advance that it is going to take
more effort to pick up the cricket ball than the balloon,
or that the cricket ball stays put whilst the balloon blows
all over the place in a wind.

He needs to be familiar with the physical experience
before we break into his play with words, let alone ques-

tions that need answers. Language *is* important, but so is silence and if we stop to think about it we know this from our own experience – do we want to be given the recipe and directions for cooking a new dish before we have fully savoured the first mouthful?

Hunt for small seashore stones in lovely shapes and colours, some very heavy, some just right to hold (but don't leave him alone with these either).

One of the most fascinating weights of all, at any age, is a plastic bag half filled with water and carefully sealed with sellotape. Hold one between your hands and feel the weight balance move and shift as you handle it. You can vary the size of the bags and the volume of water they contain. The small ones look as though they might be bubbles but feel and behave quite differently.

Clay has a particular density all its own, and many a child who is slapping, banging, pinching and poking happily has had a shock of surprise as he tried to lift it up and balance it on one hand – the wrist gives under the strain and what seemed quite a manageable lump proves it to be much heavier than it looked. Clay is a beautiful material for any age, but *only* if your toddler is comfortably in his play clothes, if he is playing where dropped pieces will do no harm, if the clay has enough water worked into it to make it pliable enough for small fingers, but not so sticky that it puts *you* off, and above all if *you* are happy to let him play. The atmosphere we create for children decides right from the start whether or not they will play fully, freely, happily and valuably.

If you can set up clay play so that you are happy about it, then your toddler will love the feel of it with his skin-feel, shape-feel and weight-feel, and as he works with his fingers, hands, wrists, arms and even neck muscles you will see the play change from being soothing to being exciting, from being fast to being slow, from the use of strong to delicate movements and back again. He will be playing fully, freely and in harmony with himself and his surroundings and this is the best play of all.

Just think, if our climate was warmer, and if we were less bound by convention our children could do what comes naturally and toddle out of doors to play naked or with the minimum of protective clothing in sand, earth, clay and mud, to their heart's content – with water too, under a watchful eye. We can't often offer them what they really need, but if we plan for it carefully we can at least offer them the experiences they need on a smaller scale.

Dough is another beautifully manipulative material, and many of us will have happy childhood memories of playing with pieces of left-over pastry before they, too, were popped in the oven. But have you ever thought of dough as an occasional play material in its own right and not associated with cooking? (A recipe for dough is given in the Appendix.) Plasticine and Playdoh are certainly no substitute for dough, and clay can only be a substitute for some children – and even then not unless it is *very* soft.

Dough is soft and silky to the touch, very responsive to the slightest pressure of the fingers, and quickly takes up the warmth of the hands. It can be wonderfully soothing and comforting or stimulating and exciting. It can be anything that a child needs it to be, and it is this that makes it such a valuable play material. Children who are tense, anxious, shy or overwrought can often find healing and peace as they clasp, knead, twist, manipulate or merely hold the soft warm inert lump. Some children will nurse and fondle a handful much as we would nurse and stroke a cat on our laps, and it does almost feel alive in its warm, soft responsiveness.

Because of this lifelike quality it is also valuable as a safe substitute for those times when a child would like to hit or pinch us or the new baby. He knows he mustn't, but so much aggression is building up inside him that it needs to be released. One such child attacked a large lump of dough saying 'I'll pinch you till you bleed!' but before

117

long the pinching and bashing had spent itself and he was playing happily.

Dough is also 'clean', and therefore the child feels 'good' in a way that sometimes isn't possible with clay, especially if we have unwittingly given him the idea that to be dirty is naughty. (We need to watch this. Is it naughty to get dirty working under the car ?)

Some of you may have scruples about using food as a play material when there is so much famine in the world, and this must be a matter for the individual conscience when other facts have been taken into consideration. Quite often the children who most need dough to calm them aren't eating very much anyway at this point, and you may feel that it is justified to give them food for their hands instead of for their mouths from time to time.

We have also created our own brand of famine in society by denying children the environment that they need for full, free development of their minds, bodies and spirits. If we deny them access to the raw materials of the world – sand, clay, earth, water, rocks and trees to climb – then we owe them substitutes, for if we cheat them of these basic experiences we are preventing their full growth just as surely as lack of food is preventing full growth in famine areas (where, ironically, children sometimes have ideal natural surroundings for play).

Water-feel

This isn't quite like anything else, and it is one of the experiences that we could give most easily, yet so often don't. 'Hurry up!' we say as our toddler lingers over handwashing. Worse still, we do it for him because we don't want the dinner to get cold, or we want to catch the bus, or we've just cleaned the basin.

It's often the same with the bath, whether it is a tin bath by the fire, the kitchen sink, or a modern bath. The day has been a long one, we're tired, a hungry man will soon be in for a meal, the kitchen is a mess, the baby needs to be topped and tailed and fed – who can blame us if we soap the toddler quickly, rinse him down and lift him out?

It was a bath-by-the-fire mother who gave me fresh thought on this matter. She was agreeing with a group of parents that the evening rush is the most difficult part of the day, and then she went on:

'So I don't bath him then. About four o'clock suits us fine. I sit down with a cup of tea, or the potatoes to peel, or with the ironing, while he plays in the bath beside me. He has a lovely time, squeezing the flannel down his tummy, and tipping cups of water down himself, and floating things, and playing with his little teapot. If I think the water's getting cold I lift him out, and top up with a kettle, and pop him back again. He's good as gold and it gives me time to have a bit of a break before it all starts happening again.'

More of us need to do this, to consider what our children really do need, and then see if we can find ways of offering it to them that will give us both a greater happiness and peace of mind than we had before.

If we plan well enough in advance hand-washing can take five or ten happy minutes with a piece of soap, a few soap flakes tipped into his wet up-turned hand, or a squirt of mild detergent that has to be stirred up to make bubbles. A sponge or nailbrush can prolong the job of work (which is also play and learning) for longer still, and you will have time to dish up in peace.

Gumboots, sticks and puddles are another happy combination. So is watering the flowers, even if it is only watering a pot plant by means of repeatedly immersing a very small bottle in a pudding basin of water (the air bubbling out of the bottle is half the fun, and the water will tip into the plant pot with a minimum of spills).

Some of us may remember the exhilaration of going out in pouring rain in bathing costumes, or nothing at all! Half the joy of this was the unexpectedness of hearing adults say 'Yes, why not?' We felt daring and excited and the sodden grass squelched under our toes, and the water trickled through our hair on to our scalps, and once we were soaking wet and acclimatised to the temperature it felt wonderful. So did the hot bath and rub-down afterwards.

Rain is life-giving, yet we so often moan about it and colour our children's attitudes when we could be learning from their pleasure in it – but first we have to allow them to experience it as a pleasure. People in drought areas know what it is to pray for rain, and then to rush out when it comes, to dance and laugh and revel in it. Our children could feel the same delight in rain that they do in sun.

In high-rise flats, bath and wash-basin may be the children's main contact with water, and at least they will not be denied the sensation of buoyancy in water, which is one of its most distinctive characteristics. But the personal experience of weather remains important, lest we cut children and ourselves off from that source of meeting nature at first hand. It takes a great effort for parents living under those conditions to say 'Let's put on our macs and our gumboots and go for a walk in the rain', but if you can find shared pleasure in such an experience you will be well on the way to helping your child to experience and accept weather naturally as part of the life-cycle rather than as a matter of personal pleasure or inconvenience.

Scribble and Daub

The impulse to scribble, daub and paint is a natural one, and that it isn't confined to children is clear as we can see from walls, posters, railway carriages and subways covered in graffiti, restaurants, churches and youth clubs adorned with murals. The growing number of art classes and exhibitions is a further indication of the pleasure people are discovering in this form of expression.

It helps a bit to remember this as we survey the occasional scribble or writing on our own walls. One child was so excited when she found she could write that the words 'Pauline' and 'Hot' were written in thick black pencil wherever she went that first day of her miraculous discovery – on the rabbit hutch, on the sloping ceiling under the stairs, on walls and doors and on sheet after sheet of toilet paper until she was discovered.

Even in the best regulated families these things are apt to happen and we scold or explain according to our degree of distress at the time, but unless we understand the strength of this natural drive we may rightly prevent it happening in the wrong places but fail to provide for it to happen legitimately elsewhere.

Children make marks on various surfaces all the time. They spill milk or fruit juice and smear it about with one finger or a sweep of the hand. Chocolatey fingers are wiped down a bib or apron and the brown marks are surveyed with interest and a good deal of surprise. Lines are traced on steamy windows, and marks are made in earth or sand with fingers or sticks.

One day we may leave a pencil within reach and our toddler discovers that there is a certain kind of stick that leaves marks that stay, and since his eyes are riveted by the marks themselves he goes on making them without being aware of what it is that he is marking. Since he isn't 'drawing' at this stage but is only interested in this new discovery he will be content with a large black pencil and a large piece of paper cut from a roll of lining paper, or a smooth piece of wrapping paper, or a newspaper that he has fetched from wherever you keep old newspapers (this habit needs to be established lest he mistakenly uses today's paper and finds himself unpopular because you haven't read it yet). The paper needs to be anchored to a smooth surface because his movements may be so vigorous that the pencil goes right through the paper, which will be frustrating for him and upsetting for you if you have heavy black marks on your lino tiles or tablecloth.

You can sellotape the paper to the underside of an old tray, or clip it with clothes pegs to a piece of hardboard, plywood or stout card. You can put the prepared mounted paper on the floor, or on a table, or prop it up firmly on the seat of a chair that acts as an easel; or the paper can be drawing-pinned safely to chipboard mounted on one particular wall that the toddler understands is for his use (but keep an eye on the drawing pins).

As you watch him scribble you will see why he needs a big sheet of paper, for the first cautious dots and dabs usually lead him into a continuous east–west movement with the pencil clutched in his fist and the ever-widening marks zigzag back and forth across the paper. The next natural progression tends to be a round and round movement, giving oval rather than circular marks, and at some stage the movement may be continuous. It may also be a series of swoops that almost but not quite joins the end of the line to the beginning. Then there may be more dots and dashes, then lines made by pushing the pencil up the sheet or across, or pulling it downwards, but all done with deliberation and deep concentration.

Scribbling is a most purposeful form of play that prepares the way for *much* later drawing and writing, but as with all stages of human growth and development nature doesn't get on with the job nearly so well if we interfere and try to hurry things up. Children need their scribbling stage, and we should be content to provide the paper and big pencils, coloured pencils, chubby wax crayons, and thick powder paint with big hog's-hair brushes in order that they may have the scope to do quite literally what comes naturally.

If you keep the scribbles you will be able to look through them later on and see for yourself how each stage follows the other until eventually there appears what looks like a face with eyes and hair, or is it a radiating sun? Whatever it is it appears spontaneously even in the work of children who have never had an adult draw for them or seen picture books.

Then the big-head sprouts arms and legs, but you will have to wait for your child's all-round development to advance a bit further before he spontaneously begins to attach a body to the head, and arms and legs to the body. It will be later still before you can recognise anything even remotely resembling a picture, and even then you may be wrong in your interpretation so it pays to say 'Tell me about it' when it is presented to you lest you make the sad mistake I made one day by saying 'What a lovely bunch of bananas.' The child's face fell as he said 'It's not a bunch of bananas, it's a mummy bird and the baby birds and their auntie on a swing.'

Children's imaginations and fantasies are so much richer than ours and we need to be sensitive if we are not to blunt them; it pays to be careful if they say 'Draw me a house.' It may be more rewarding to say to them 'You draw me a house instead. Whose house will it be?'

We may be surprised to learn how much our child already remembers about where people live – in flats, in a house with another one joined on to it, in a house surrounded by a garden, even in a caravan. We may also be intrigued to find that sometimes the child will talk and draw simultaneously, but the result may be extremely odd from our point of view. One child said she would draw Granny's house, and announced that it had a door (which she drew at the top of the page), and lots of windows (which were drawn in a line across the page under the door), and pretty curtains (which were coloured spots and scribbles in another line under the windows). She recalled and recorded all the facts as she remembered them and was vastly pleased with the result, which although it in no way resembled a house to look at had clearly brought both Granny and her house vividly alive in her imagination at that point. (See page 243 for details of *What's a House?*, a book of children's paintings, with explanations, and advice on setting up a home painting corner.)

If your child can be encouraged naturally and easily to enjoy scribbling, drawing and painting you will be providing for hours of valuable play which will be a source of great pleasure to you as well: and if you keep the results in chronological order you will have a visual record of one of the growing-up processes to which all spontaneous play contributes. You will also benefit from the lengthening spells of his quiet and concentrated periods of play and there is no need to feel guilty because you revel in such peace and quiet occasionally.

Once your child has discovered this particular joy it pays to make or buy an easel, and to keep it easily available with paint ready mixed in spillproof containers, complete with a brush in each, and clean paper clipped on ready for action. Alternatively, fix a scribbling board to his bedroom or the kitchen wall.

The love of painting springs from a recognition of the need to paint, and as the interest develops it can be encouraged still further by the provision of sheets of sugar paper (stronger and more absorbent than lining paper or newspaper) or coloured art paper, together with the introduction of new colours, and black or white to mix with them to give new shades.

Another happy form of 'painting' is to offer a small

bucket or bowl of water (stay near enough to keep an eye on this for safety's sake) and a decorator's brush or roller to be used on a concrete or paved path, a brick wall or fence, or a flat's balcony. The water makes satisfying trail marks, leaves no mess, and dries quickly enough to invite more painting quite soon.

Undisciplined scribblers can be a menace in any home, but if you recognise this as the first stage in a new and valuable phase of growth and development you can encourage it in a positive way, and congratulate yourself on having recognised it in time to be able to set sail with the tide instead of cutting across it and running into squalls.

Part 3
Living Together

Daily Routines

There can be no such thing as a daily routine that applies to everyone, especially since your home may be in a high-rise flat, on a farm, in one or two rooms, in a house with a garden, in a caravan, or in a seaside house where you work all the hours there are during the summer taking in visitors.

In addition to the differences in living accommodation, some mothers may be married to shift workers, some may have schoolchildren and possibly a baby in addition to a toddler, some may have a handicapped child or be handicapped, and some have to cope on their own.

Even more important, each of you is different and this counts even more than the difference in circumstances. You may be highly organised, or casually half-organised, or cheerfully chaotic. You may be predominantly intellectual, or emotional, or a happy medium. You may love every minute of being a parent, even when sheer tiredness makes the going hard, or you may feel frustrated and long to hand the job over to someone else. You may be familiar with children, or they may be new to you and baffling in their inability to think, reason and behave as you expected they could and would.

A family's circumstances can be so very different, and yet all toddlers have the same needs. Toddlers need food, warmth, shelter, fresh air and exercise, love that is warm and accepting yet sets limits, predictability in people and events, and an environment and relationships that make it possible to learn through doing and being and playing throughout each day.

The most predictable routine events for your toddler are probably dressing, washing, mealtimes and bedtime, to which most will be able to add going out. The most predictable events for you are probably cooking, washing-up, bedmaking, cleaning, washing, ironing, shopping and the everlasting tidying (or the everlasting search for things because there hasn't been time for tidying). And looking after a toddler comes on top of all that.

This is often the real stumbling-block. We devise and adopt a daily routine that suits our pre-child state, and then try to fit the child into the routine without trying to see how it must seem to him.

We may see the dressing, washing and mealtime routines as something to be got through in order to get to the in-between bits, which we think of as our work time and the child's play time. If he could tell us how this same plan seemed to him he might say: 'Well, there are times when I get bundled about a bit, and they say "Come on . . . hurry up . . . quickly." Sometimes in between the hurry ups it's "Hand in here . . . now leg . . .", and sometimes it's "open . . . and another . . . don't spill . . .". Then it's "You play with your toys while I just do this", and after all that hurry there's ages when I have nothing to do and I get fed up. And if I find something to do it's almost always wrong, and if I want to be played with it's "I'll come in a minute." A minute must be the longest thing in the world. And why do they think that play is toys?'

The routines that we try to get through so quickly and efficiently are the very stuff of a toddler's learning, for which time is needed, but if you think about the dressing, washing and mealtime rituals from his point of view you will find ways of extending his idea of play without any detriment to your day's work at all. In fact the rethinking, not so much of the routine itself but of your attitude to it, will make your life very much easier, with the added bonus that the more you are able to integrate your work of bringing him up, his play, and your daily tasks the more you will find you are enjoying each other. In those rare moments when the three come perfectly together you will suddenly understand the meaning of the profound statement 'A child's play is his work', for you will have discovered that your work has the happiness and satisfaction of play.

In reconsidering your attitude to each day you will probably find that one of the biggest stumbling-blocks is that you are dependent on the clock while your child has no sense of clock-time at all, but is dependent on development-time. The real lesson that has to be learned is just how much time to allow for a child at the toddler stage to accomplish each apparently simple task, for only then is it possible to gear clock-time to development-time so that life flows more smoothly.

Dressing

If you saw an advertisement for a toy proclaiming 'Fascinating! Fun! Safe! Hygienic! Guarantees, literally hours of educational play for your toddler at a give-away price!' would you be tempted to buy it?

The chances are he already has one, it's called a vest.

Hundreds of times, literally, you have pulled something soft and dark over your baby's head, and eased his fists and arms through two holes, and made his tummy feel warm as part of the dressing ritual. You may even have put his pram under the clothes line so that he could watch coloured shapes hang limply or toss and twist in the wind, but he couldn't possibly make the connection between one of these things and the thing you so deftly pull over his head and arms each day.

With luck you won't have missed the magical moment when a toddler picks his vest up from the chair and for the first time *knows* that it is a vest. At last he has made the connection between the word he has heard so many times, the physical sensations that usually accompany the word, and this small object that he has picked up not just with recognition but with the intention of doing for himself what you have done for him in the past.

But this isn't easy. He knows that something goes over his head first, but he is quite likely to plonk it on top of his head with the expectation that the next bit happens by itself. When it doesn't he may remove it and have a good hard look at the uncooperative object. He then probably lifts it to his head again, holding a handful above each ear, and pulls downwards firmly until he is wearing a sort of bonnet. It feels warm and does something funny to his hearing, but still doesn't do what he knows it should do if it really is a vest.

Another inspection may reveal a hole through which a

hand may be inserted, and hope returns briefly before frustration sets in. A vest has four holes. And when you pick a hole up it often stops looking like a hole and you don't know where it's gone. At this point wouldn't you feel like giving up and crying with frustration, or try to comfort your chilly inadequate self with a good thumb-sucking?

On this first occasion he may be glad when you come to the rescue and put it on for him, but the next day he will try again – and again and again – oblivious of the fact that you are trying to dress yourself, leave the bathroom free in good time for others who need to use it, get the milk in, put the cat out, cook and serve breakfast, and get him washed, dressed and safely into his special seat for breakfast.

If you had time to see and understand what was going on you might say to yourself: 'What tenacity, what courage, what optimism, what a breakthrough from dependence towards independence, what a lot he has already learned, and what a lot he still hasn't understood!' But in your early morning rush it is very understandable if you say 'Here, over your head, now your hand, quickly', and then it is even more understandable if he yells with frustration, while you become tight-lipped and determined as you dress him and carry him down to join the family for breakfast on time.

Your early morning pattern may be quite different, but the constant factor is that at some point your child will want to learn how to dress himself, and you will want him to be able to. So how, when and where can the stage be set for the learning process, bearing in mind that it is going to be a fascinating, challenging and time-consuming business for *both* of you?

He will need to be warm, you will need to be comfortable, and both of you will need to be peaceful. You wouldn't want a driving lesson to be rushed and harassed, and an assortment of clothes is just as complicated as an assortment of gears and knobs. You may dislike dressing gowns at the breakfast table, but for a while it may be best to postpone dressing until the morning rush is over. You may both have breakfast in dressing gowns anyway, so afterwards he can experiment while you dress, and by then he may be ready to be helped. You may be an early riser and prefer to help him slowly before breakfast. He may be a late sleeper so that the family breakfast is over when he wakes, and he can start the day slowly and satisfyingly by applying himself to the serious business of getting up 'properly', with you at hand to encourage and help unobtrusively.

It doesn't matter when or where he gets dressed at this stage. What matters is that you should take pride in his readiness to learn *and your recognition of it* – and if you have this degree of sensitivity and awareness you will also have the flexibility to find the time and place to take the opportunity that has presented itself. Learning to dress is the absorbing sort of work that really is 'child's play' as far as he is concerned, and if you are calm and allow yourself enough time you will find it quite a challenge to your imagination to devise the simplest and most foolproof way of teaching him how to put on each garment, and how to master the art of putting a button and a hole together in such a way that they fasten two pieces of material together.

If he will accept direct help, try sitting on a low chair with his vest face-down on your lap, the neck towards you and the body stretched down to your knees. You can then lift up the top layer of the hem so that he begins to see the tunnel into which he needs to put his arms to find the armholes, and then you can help him to put his head through the middle hole. You may evolve a different system, but whatever it is it needs to be one that can be learned and followed – whether the vest is laid out on your lap, on a chair or on the floor – and one that takes into consideration that the garment needs to be the right way round at the end of it all, for although this doesn't matter too much in the case of a vest it certainly does matter when it comes to trousers.

The repetition of the system will need to go on for several days probably, though with increasing independence. By this time you may both think it a good idea for you to be doing something else simultaneously in the same room, so that you are on hand to offer praise, encouragement or the odd reminder without his feeling crowded or hustled. You can clean the bath, make the bed, wash up or do whatever comes naturally according to the room that has been chosen as the warmest and most suitable one for this particular stage of learning.

There usually comes another stage when there is no longer the need for quite such a depth of concentration but when the new-found speed and ease give rise to a slip and the garment goes on inside out or back to front. It is best to turn a blind eye to this. How do you like it if you have cleaned three windows and someone comes in and points out that you haven't cleaned the fourth one yet? However, if he notices and pauses for consideration you might say 'It's all right, it's just back to front. Would you like to leave it, or shall we change it?' Abide by his decision. The preface 'It's all right, it's only . . .' is a helpful one. It builds up self-esteem whereas 'You've got it back to front' implies a criticism which either leads to loss of confidence or to a fierce desire to save face by refusing point-blank to change anything.

If it is trousers that are back to front it will probably be uncomfortable to sit down, let alone anything else, and if he is clearly uncomfortable you can save face by saying, 'Let's have a look at those trousers, are they getting a bit small for you? No, I know what it is, the back's got to the front and the front's got to the back!' There isn't any need to rub it in that *he* got them back to front, and if you can laugh together at the back-to-frontness it is easy to say, 'What shall we do? Leave them as they are

135

or take them off and turn them round?' Abide by his decision if he says 'Leave them', and try to refrain from having the last word along the lines of 'You'll be uncomfortable!'

Each time he masters a new skill he may want to go on practising just for the joy of it, and you may be able to extend this form of play to meet his need. If he has just mastered buttons and buttonholes he may like three different-sized cardigans stuffed with three cushions, then you can iron peacefully (after all the ironing has got to be done) whilst starting him off with the idea that it is a very cold day and the little old lady and the big fat man and their dog need to be buttoned up in their cardigans to keep them warm. This is buttoning with a purpose, which adds to the pleasure, and often the concentration span can be quite long, though you will need to say at intervals 'The sun's coming out, and it's getting warmer and warmer and now the poor man is too hot!' (or cold, or wet – which means a variation of the play as he takes it off and brings it to you to 'iron dry'). The happier the learning experience has been for both of you the longer and more rewarding the following spells of imaginative play will be.

As with other stages of development independent dressing brings its own problems. There is almost bound to come a day when you are both going shopping or to visit someone rather special, and to your consternation your toddler has quietly dressed himself to give you a surprise. His buttons are wrongly matched to their buttonholes so that his coat is poking up round one ear and drabbling down to the opposite knee, his beret is round his eyebrows, and his face is beaming with pride and joy.

What do you do? You will both be very privileged if you can smile back and say 'We're ready, off we go!' without turning a hair. You will be human if you find yourself saying 'Look at you! You can't go out like that, come here . . . stand still a minute' and, having done his coat, if you pull his beret off, smooth his hair with your fingers and put it on again at your preferred angle.

You will also be human if you start out together confidently without adjusting his clothes, and then lose your nerve when you meet people you know and start to apologise for your child in front of him 'Look at him! He got dressed himself to give me a surprise, and I didn't have the heart to do anything about it.' You will be superb if you meet your acquaintances as though nothing were amiss, and if they should so far forget their good manners as to comment 'Look at him, what's he been up to?' you reply warmly, 'He got dressed to come out all by himself *and* he got dressed by himself this morning — vest, pants, trousers, T-shirt, socks, shoes, everything!'

Children are persons, with feelings and dignity, and we owe them all the common courtesies that we hope for ourselves.

Washing

There is a difference of opinion between adults and children as to the nature and purpose of washing.

Adults usually acquire the habit in early childhood and although enthusiasm for the idea wanes somewhat a few years later it is eventually reinforced by the discovery that it is widely accepted and expected outside their own homes, and by a growing understanding of the connection between health and hygiene.

Each of us has a unique collection of memories of how, when and where we were washed and bathed in childhood. The predominant memory may be of a painted and chipped iron bath in a freezing bathroom, a shared tap on a tenement landing, a kitchen sink, a tin bath filled by water drawn from a well and heated in the outhouse copper, an enamelled or plastic bowl on a low bench, or a matching pastel bath and pedestal basin in a heated bathroom. Recall as many memories as you can of when and where you were washed, and as they come back to you they will bring with them memories of who and how and why.

As you look back you may find that along with the habit of washing you acquired certain attitudes, one of which may be the association of dirtiness with naughtiness and cleanliness with goodness. The association of words and feelings affects us all to some extent but before handing on our habits and attitudes to our children we need to think about our motives for asking children to wash at intervals throughout each day, and then to try to see the child's point of view.

'Now let's wash our hands' we say after helping a child in the lavatory, and the 'we' gives a comfortable feeling of togetherness that makes the washing as natural as the emptying of the bladder or bowel.

You will all have your own standard of hygiene on this matter: some will enforce the rule, reasoning that a habit isn't formed unless it is made a rule; some may enforce it through a real fear of infection and a talk with your health visitor or doctor may help you to find a better balance between fear and sensible precaution. Some of you will quietly insist on washing after the emptying of the bowel, but turn a blind eye occasionally if a child wriggles uncomfortably at his play then trots off to the lavatory only to return with washless speed. You may feel that if you send him back for a wash he will resent the break in his play so much that next time he will deny the call of nature until it is too late. There is no 'right' answer because each of you has to balance what you feel to be right from the hygienic point of view with what you feel to be right for your particular toddler at each stage in his development.

Whether or not you are rigid in your handwashing training you may find that once a habit is established some children are distressed if circumstances make it impossible to carry it out, and sometimes it is necessary to find a symbolic substitute. For example, if the water supply has run out on a picnic then a 'wash' with a handful of grass or a hankie is more helpful than 'Don't make a fuss' or 'You can't eat anything else until we get home and you have a wash'. Emotional health is just as important as physical health and it would be as sad to make children unhealthily germ-conscious as it would be insensitive to a present need not to make a token gesture to certain established rituals.

'Come and get washed for dinner' is another familiar cry for which there may be several reasons in addition to that of hygiene. At a practical level it makes extra work if dirty hands soil tablecloths or tops, bibs and chairs, and aesthetically it is an unattractive contrast to see grime added to the dampness of mugs and transferred everywhere within reach when the table has been attractively laid. But deeper down than this most of us who spend a great deal of our lives in the selecting, buying, carrying, preparing and cooking of food want and need the satisfaction of seeing the meal enjoyed and appreciated, and in this context the washing of children's hands is not just hygienic or expedient but a ritual of preparation and anticipation prior to receiving something that has been specially prepared for them.

Again, you will all have differing views on this, and some providers of meals may be quite content to see the family swoop down, dishevelled and none too clean, and clear the decks before rushing off again. If you are one of these spare a thought for others who may have to provide your family with food, including future wives and husbands.

A student who was a waitress during one summer holiday said how demoralising it was to discover that almost no one saw her as a person; she was just 'the thing that brought the food'. Appreciation of a meal, or a clean car, or a bowl of flowers, or the mending of something, only comes about if we set the scene in such a way that even very young children can 'see' what is before them and this comes about as they sense the value that we put upon our own and other people's work, and as we offer them the experience of sharing this same work. They will then begin to feel the satisfaction of doing a job for its own sake, and to discover that appreciation adds an extra dimension of pleasure.

The washing period before a meal gives a child time to let go of the last play activity and to prepare mentally as well as physically for the meal that is to be put before him, whether it is baked beans on toast or a three-course meal with all the trimmings.

All this is easy enough to say, but even if you agree with the thinking it still isn't easy to judge the timing: if a child is brought to the table before the food is ready life becomes difficult for everyone; if you are stirring sauce-

pans and keeping an eye on the oven you can't leave it
for a leisurely washing session; if you send him to wash
alone he disappears for ages and leaves soggy soap and
towels behind him. You can't suggest a wash at the sink
if it is full of pots and pans, and if you wipe his hands
quickly with his special kitchen flannel you know that it
isn't helping him to learn about handwashing.

As always it is a matter of compromise; the constant
factor is the need to wash before meals and the when,
where and how of it has to be balanced according to
circumstances. Another constant factor is that children
almost always need much more time than we allow them,
to which you may well reply, 'But if I give him more
time he just plays about.' Therein lies the heart of the
matter for what is playing-about to adults is playing-to-
learn for children.

Imagine the handwashing business from the child's
point of view. He knows you pull up his sleeves, so he
grabs a handful of sleeve at the elbow and heaves. Nothing
happens because the pull is often outwards instead of
upwards, or he pulls upwards but the shirt sleeve is still
buttoned, or the ribbing of the jumper is tight, or the
pull isn't strong enough to bring his cuffs well back from
his wrists where he knows they should be. He tries running
one hand from his wrist to his elbow, but nothing happens
for him although when you do it the sleeve wrinkles up to
the elbow in a most miraculous way leaving his arm bare.

The chances are that having battled unsuccessfully
with his sleeves he will give up and methodically go on to
the next bit, which is putting the plug in the plughole –
but the chain may be twisted round the tap and he hasn't
yet learned to tell just by looking which way round it is
twisted. He may twist and twist until there is no chain
left free, then he may try in the opposite direction until
the whole length snakes down into the bowl.

It all takes time.

Hopefully you will have been *very* careful to teach him

which tap is hot and which is cold, and slowly he turns the tap or taps as you have shown him. Sometimes a fierce flow of water will dislodge the plug, water pours away as fast as it flows, his fingers aren't strong enough to refit the plug under the waterfall, and his anxious eye is so riveted on the plug and plughole that he can't yet think to turn the tap off and start again. If you can remember the panic of trying to replace a plug under such circumstances, or of trying in vain to turn off a tap that was stuck at full gush, then it is easy to say 'It's all right, I'll help . . . there!' rather than 'Look what you're doing!'

Once the water is in the basin the serious business of washing begins, only there are so many interesting things to see and do along the way. The soap may shoot out of his hands as he squeezes it tight for safety, and this is so surprising that he needs to do it several more times to try to understand such a strange contradiction; or it may be pale and slimy underneath, tempting him to scrape little runnels with his fingertips or to scrape all the soft soap away in order to make it dark and hard all over.

Suddenly the clear water has gone and he can't see the plug any longer, and his hands disappear too if he puts them in deep enough – only now his sleeves are wet because he hadn't eyes for that bit of his arm until it was too late.

Even the process of rubbing soapy hands together is fascinating, for it can be done in so many ways – up and down, round and round, with fingers interlocking to show all his nails or interlocking to hide them, or one hand removing all the soap from the other, and then the other getting it all back again. Watch yourself washing your own hands just for once and rediscover how varied and interesting the movements are, for then you will begin to understand how much you do automatically that a child has to learn through personal experience.

You are probably wanting him to get through washing to get to dinner, but he finds getting to and getting through washing a major operation in its own right. You won't always be able to be patient and slow, but on those occasions when you can you will find it a pleasure to share his learning.

Mothers shut up alone with a toddler all day often say 'The day is so long, and he doesn't know what to do with himself most of the time', so it is in the interest of you both to give full value to *all* the events of the day, and if your child can spend ten very happy and valuable learning minutes washing his hands then be glad for both your sakes, and just allow that much time before each meal while the interest lasts.

'Just look at your hands! Go and wash them' is another familiar cry, and this usually means 'Get that dirt off before it transfers itself to everything in sight' rather than 'Be careful of the germs.' This is the cry that needs most thought because so often it conveys to the child that you don't approve either of his dirt or him, when if you stopped to think about it you might find that you did approve of him and his dirty state but were rightly concerned about where he put his dirtiness. For example, if the family wage earner is a garage mechanic then he will have some very dirty clothes to be washed, but that doesn't make him a 'bad boy': he is a 'good boy' who has been working hard, in the process of which his clothes have become dirty. The dirtiness is accepted as inevitable, and the area for discussion centres round where the clothes can reasonably be worn indoors, where they are removed, and where they are kept pending washing.

As a farmer's daughter I learned that muddy gumboots were left in the scullery, wet socks and macs went through to the kitchen to dry; the first washing if hands were caked in mud took place under the pump in the stone sink in the scullery, the second wash took place in the kitchen sink – but anyone brought in to have first aid was taken straight to the kitchen no matter what the state of his or her boots. It was taken for granted that men and women couldn't work or children play outside without getting dirty.

Nothing can alter the fact that children need to be dirty and messy as well as clean, any more than it can alter the fact that many parents were brought up to react strongly against mess and dirt. The problem is how to reconcile these opposites. What miraculously can and does happen is that very often parents are able to rethink and relearn their attitudes as they watch their children if they can recall what it felt like to do those same things in their own childhood.

I have listened to so many parents recalling their earliest play memories of mud-pies, scraping moss or mortar from between bricks, stirring up muddy puddles with sticks, playing on builders' sand (which stained their clothes orange), making 'mixtures' of salt, vinegar, flour, gravy browning, jam, sugar, currants and anything else that came to hand. And, as they recall how it 'felt' to do all these things, so inevitably they recall their parents' attitudes: 'Dad belted us one'; 'Mum used to moan but she never minded too much'; 'Mother used to say "As long as you're clean to start the day, and clean to end it, I don't mind what you do in between" '; 'Our parents never minded us getting dirty as long as we didn't trail it all over the house'; 'We were never allowed to get dirty, and I feel worried even now if my hands are dirty and I just can't bear the feel of earth on them'; 'My father used to say to my mother "It's nothing that a good wash won't put right" and then mother would simmer down'.

One of the agreed best memories of parents is of those times when the joy of really happy, purposeful, inventive play was suddenly marred by the realisation of how dirty and dishevelled they had become, and they went in at the back door expecting trouble only to have their joy restored by the totally unexpected greeting: 'You look as though you've had a lovely time, what have you been doing?'

If you know that you err on the side of being over-houseproud, try to train yourself to look at your child's face before you say anything about the mess he's in. He just may have been cleaning your bicycle wheels with a hankie as a lovely and loving surprise for you, and you will be glad that you managed to say 'Hello! what have you been doing?' before exclaiming about the state he's in.

'Come on, time for bed' is the last call of the day to wash or bath, but bedtime is a routine that needs special consideration in its own right and we'll come to that later.

Since washing is part of toilet training this section wouldn't really be complete without mentioning bladder and bowel control, and how we contribute to a toddler's sense of success or failure. This is a matter of joint learning rather than of one 'training' the other. I well remember one mother's anxiety because her baby wasn't 'trained' at the age of nine months, and another mother who felt exasperated because her eighteen-month-old son wouldn't wee in his potty. 'He stands there with his trousers down, and I kneel there holding the potty under him and say "Come on, then", but he just won't – and then as soon as his trousers are back on again they're wet!'

Many young parents don't realise that small boys can't stand up to urinate before they have a high degree of control over their bladders, and that whilst they and little girls are trying to acquire this control they need to sit in a relaxed position. At first it is sheer luck, or the stimulation of contact with the potty, if either their bladders or bowels work, but gradually they come to associate adult approval with this particular happening and very slowly their muscular control and their desire to please develop together.

Some of you will have children who by the toddler stage are dry by day and even by night, which you may attribute to the fact that you have been potting them for a few quiet moments at regular intervals during the day and night since they were born. Others will have similarly

145

dry toddlers, which you may attribute to the fact that you made no attempt to pot them until they were two years old or even later! Others may have toddlers who are still in nappies that appear to be constantly wet or dirty, and again some of you will have potted regularly and some not at all. Others will have toddlers who are reliably clean and dry during the day but almost never during the night.

If you have a wet and dirty toddler don't worry about the past, just accept that it is so at the moment and start from there.

First understand how difficult it is to control the muscles of the bladder and anus – even for us. You may be able to recall a visit to the surgery or hospital when you were given a bottle and told to produce a sample then and there, and you may have found it impossible to release the muscles at will. In an attempt to help you a tap may have been turned on, and sometimes the gush of water brought about the desired result, but sometimes not even that helped. You may have travelled abroad in places where a hole in the floor replaces our pedestal lavatories, and again found that your muscles wouldn't easily obey your will. How much more difficult, then, for children to learn to control muscles hidden inside themselves that have been working for months without any conscious effort on their part at all. If this difficulty has been heightened by your impatience or anger, then these feelings need to be acknowledged as a first step towards controlling them – which may be as difficult for you as the muscular control will be for him. You are in this together and need to forgive each other and start again.

You may feel it is best to forget the pot for a while and just change him kindly and cheerfully when he is uncomfortable. If you do pot him let it be an unhurried operation (remembering how difficult it is to release the muscles to order) but don't leave him sitting for more than a minute or so once he is relaxed. Some parents have found it helpful to go to the lavatory together with their toddler so that it is something that 'we' do rather than 'I am waiting for you to do', but embarrassment may make this impossible for others.

A warm potty is more conducive to relaxed muscles than a cold one, and one that fits comfortably rather than one that is too small or too large. Sometimes it helps to buy a new one anyway and let the toddler throw the old one in the dustbin (together with his anxiety related to it with any luck). If he uses the lavatory then he will feel safer on a child's adjustable seat fitted over the existing one than being held on by you; he will also feel more relaxed if his feet are firmly on a stool or polythene grow-tall step (for standing to wash at the basin afterwards, too).

The words 'comfy' and 'uncomfy' are more helpful than 'dry' and 'wet' when changing is necessary, they convey that you are concerned about how he *feels* about the state he is in rather than the state itself. If he associates the word 'comfy' with pleasant memories such as being comfy on your lap to be read to, and comfy tucked up in a warm bed, then it may begin to dawn on him that this 'comfy' thing is worth cultivating. Words and their meaning reinforce each other helpfully – 'Are you uncomfy? Let's make you nice and dry', followed by 'There! all warm and dry again. Is that nice and comfy?' The same comfort principle often works well over the nappies themselves, and many a mother has found it works to say on a beautiful day, 'I don't think you want those old nappies on a lovely day like this, do you? Let's put on your knickers/pants and then you can come running in quickly if you want the potty and it won't take a minute!' But try to catch him in time to reinforce the joy of the nappyless state. One mother of a perpetually wet three-year-old suggested this, which had the desired effect immediately, and she said with sudden insight, 'Do you know, I've only just seen that until that minute she hadn't realised that nappies weren't for wetting!'

147

Children differ greatly in their bladder control, and also in the amount of liquid they drink. Some children pass a little at frequent intervals, some hold it longer and pass more, and it doesn't necessarily follow that the first group have weak bladders and the second group are holding on harmfully – though both those things may be true occasionally.

Even children who are normally dry can have lapses. Playing with water often causes them to react as we may have done to a running tap, so it is best to suggest a visit to the lavatory before any type of water play begins. Sleep can be so heavy that the warning signals aren't registered, or in a half-waking state a child may dream that he has got out of bed and potted himself (this can also happen at a much older stage). Excitement can either cause a lapse, or else produce false warning signals – no sooner was one of our children on a bus, just settled into the middle of a row at the pantomime, or trying on new shoes than there was a genuinely distressed cry of 'I want to spend a penny, *now* quick!', and although she had been taken a few minutes before we had to go again for the distress was too great to be born if 'in a minute' was suggested. But eventually the phase passed. If an outing or event is almost certain to produce wet pants it is demoralising to be put back in nappies, but distressing to fall from grace in public, so a happy compromise is two pairs of pants with a nappy liner between them.

Dryness at night takes longer, especially with deep sleepers, but sometimes it can be accomplished when the time comes to transfer from a cot to a bed. There can be a gentle and unobtrusive build-up towards this by praise for a dry cot and the comment 'Soon you will be ready for a big bed!' When the transfer takes place, obviously a waterproof undersheet will be needed as a precaution for many months, and a draw sheet too so that the washing isn't heavier than it has been in the cot in the event of a wet night. Potting when you go to bed may make for success, but not if you have a light sleeper who will not only wake up but also keep you awake for hours.

Success can be reinforced and encouraged sometimes by new sheets or pillowcases or new and rather special pyjamas or nighties – our son chose his own material and watched me make a scarlet pair, an emerald pair, and his favourite 'stripey tigers' of green, yellow, maroon, blue and goodness knows what else. They worked like a magic charm.

A bedtime teddy can have his own nappies (if this is agreeable to your toddler, but not otherwise) and your toddler may be able to tell you, via Ted, how he feels about things – 'He doesn't want silly old nappies any more' or 'He's naughty and wet and I've spanked him very hard'. This probably means: 'I was wet last night, and I feel very bad about it – I shan't tell you how bad, and I hope you won't say much now that you know I feel it was bad.' Your answer can be 'Poor Ted, I expect it was an accident and everybody has an accident now and again, so let's just make him comfy and put nice clean sheets on the bed.'

If you feel you have a real problem, then talk it over with your health visitor or doctor – but I do assure you that it is very rare for a child to go to school in nappies!

Mealtimes

If your toddler eats everything with relish, just enough but not too much, and if his table manners are naturally delightful, and if he sits happily most days while you finish your meal, but you have the good sense to let him get down earlier when circumstances suggest that this would be wise and kind without being weak – then you don't need this section.

If you are frantic with worry because your child eats nothing, or exists on a diet of tomato ketchup on bread or potato crisps, if meals are a prolonged agony of 'One spoonful for Granny . . . now one for Auntie . . . now one for Fido . . . and just a tiny one for the little bird outside', then you may be comforted to know that you are not alone. It is easy enough to say 'Don't worry, it will pass', but I know from experience that it isn't possible to be a parent and not to worry about a child who isn't eating.

Most toddlers fall somewhere between the two extremes, but it may be helpful to know just how widely they vary in their eating habits at this stage. Some babies feed themselves quite well before their first birthday, others are very much slower. Some children are very slow eaters: they look around, and dream a bit, then have another mouthful, then stop eating suddenly to glance at something that has caught their attention. They may sit and look at their food with complete lack of interest, or they may keep eating steadily but very, very slowly, or they may just hold the food in their mouths.

Gentle encouragement now and again may help, or even feeding him for the last few spoonfuls as you quicken his interest in the next event, which may be pudding or going for a walk. Try not to pressure or nag, for it rarely helps. Just accept that he is slow.

Sometimes there is a turning-point of quite dramatic

speed-up triggered perhaps by a friend of his own age coming to tea (especially if the two of them have a little table or a picnic rug to themselves). Sometimes the process is gradual. Sometimes slow children grow up quite naturally to be slow adults. And very often indeed a slow child and a slow granny eat gratefully and comfortably together.

Some children are just the opposite and food is shovelled in with zest, or they will discard the spoon in favour of their hands. Before you say no too quickly to the use of hands, just stop to consider how you would feel if you were very hungry and had put before you a wonderful plate of food – and chopsticks. Eating with an unaccustomed implement is tantalisingly slow and even if the use of hands needs to be discouraged it should be done with sympathetic understanding.

If you watch a clumsy eater carefully you may see that he needs a smaller, bigger or shorter spoon, or he may be holding the spoon so uncomfortably that it is hurting his fingers. A change of implement or helping him to change his grip on the present one may help.

Sometimes it is enough to say 'Slowly', but the word needs to be said slowly and quietly, with your hand moving slowly to guide his hand slowly. If you say 'Slowly' quickly or loudly he won't know where he is, for he is still at the stage of having to rely on 'feel' to pick up the sense of words accurately.

Some children eat well, but are terribly messy in the process; and although this is perfectly natural, some parents find themselves struggling between understanding and a feeling of physical revulsion. If you are one of these, do try to resist the urge to wipe his sticky hands and mouth too many times during the course of the meal. The phase will pass and the less interference there is between a child and the enjoyment of his food the better.

Looking back over the years I can see clearly how much easier it was to cope with other people's children than our own, for the very simple reason that it was possible to act in the child's best interest calmly and unemotionally. In addition to reassuring mothers who feel they have real difficulties that their problems will almost certainly eventually resolve themselves, I hope it may be helpful if I tell you a little about children I have come across myself with similar and not uncommon difficulties in the hope that someone somewhere may light upon something helpful.

Most of these children were three or four, but it is sometimes helpful to look ahead in order to see more clearly where present attitudes might be modified to advantage.

In the days when I looked after other people's children in various types of day and residential care it wasn't unusual for a parent to hand over a new child saying, 'You'll have an awful time with his food, he doesn't eat a thing.' I would say reassuringly that he looked very well, to which the usual reply was 'Well, he'll drink milk, pints of it, so we get as much down him as we can.'

These children rarely posed a problem. For their first breakfast they would be offered the same food as everybody else, and as much milk as they wanted like everybody else, but there was no pressure or even encouragement to eat anything if they didn't want to. In the middle of the morning they would be offered orange juice and a biscuit, again with no pressure to accept either, and by the second or third day they would feel sufficiently at home to ask for milk instead. The answer to this was a friendly explanation: 'We don't have milk at this time of the day, we have orange juice – would you like to pour it out?' This sometimes led to their pouring out and drinking their own as part of the pouring ceremony.

At lunch time a small meal would be put in front of them, but an anxious look or a nod of refusal was always met with a reassuring 'It's all right, you don't have to eat it if you don't want to', and the untouched food would be removed as naturally and easily as everyone else's empty plate before the same thing happened with the pudding. At tea time no one commented if the sandwiches were uneaten, and there was again unlimited milk.

Anxious parents invariably met them in the evening with the words: 'Have you been a good boy? Did you eat up your dinner?' To save the embarrassment of the reply I would say truthfully how he had been all day (which was usually quiet but interested in everything), and add that no one expected people to eat much when everything was so new, that we didn't mind in the least, and that he had enjoyed his milk.

The important element with these children was the building up of a loving, trusting relationship that had nothing whatever to do with their eating or not eating. There was never any emotional blackmail along the lines of 'Won't you eat a little bit just to please me?' No one had to eat to please any of us; we loved them all just as they were.

The non-eaters most needed a loving relationship that took no special notice of the food issue at all – or pretended not to, because watchful eyes of course noted progress and no child would have been allowed to waste away. Once mealtimes became casual take-it-or-leave-it affairs these children began to copy the others for they no longer felt tense at mealtimes, they had nothing to gain by holding out, and something to lose judging by the pleasure with which the other children tucked into their food.

Parents sometimes felt hurt that someone else had succeeded where they had failed, and a great deal of reassurance was necessary. A baby's life depends upon its mother supplying food and she needs to know that her worry is understandable when feeding becomes difficult, that nobody blames her, and she most certainly shouldn't blame herself. Neither should parents feel that their child is deliberately playing them up. Toddlers haven't the mental equipment to work out a deliberate plan of campaign along the lines of 'I'm bored, what shall I do today? I know, I'll work mum up into one of her frenzies. Wonder what she'll do today? Coax me on her knee? Make me sit in the highchair till I've eaten it all up (only she can't *make* me eat). Weep a bit? I'll pat her cheek if she does that and then we'll cuddle each other. Scream and shout? Hit me? I don't like that, but it doesn't happen often anyway. Well, here goes, let's see!'

Usually parents can't really trace how or why it all began, but they are suddenly aware of the fact that they are beginning to feel tense and anxious as mealtimes approach. Even if nothing is said the tension communicates itself, and few things put anyone off their food quicker than tension in the air. After a while the habit of non-eating establishes itself, and even when the tension is relieved the habit may carry on for a while. If there is a change of environment to one without tension new habits can be formed, but if the people in the new environment also become tense and anxious then the child becomes trapped in the habit and comes to think that all meals everywhere have this effect on him.

If the habit is broken in a new environment, and the parents are reassured that they weren't to blame, then it isn't usually long before the new eating habit is transferred to the home. During this period the parents also need to be reassured that it doesn't matter if their child doesn't start to eat immediately, for it takes a little time for him to get used to the fact that his parents are relaxed about meals now.

As long as he is eating satisfactorily elsewhere the parents can safely adopt the policy of cutting out the extra milk, and just offer their own meals as naturally as they are being offered in the other establishment. Once parents sense that all is going to be well then, and only then, are they able to take a genuinely casual 'Eat it or not, love, it doesn't matter' attitude. Sometimes this attitude can be established in the home without recourse to outside help; it is the attitude of the parents to the problem that is all important.

Occasionally matters go further than this. In fact, once, when I was working in a wartime nursery, one child was handed over with the words 'I'd better warn you, he's sick every time he eats.' He was, too. He was thin and lacking in energy but intensely interested in the other children at a distance, and very loving and trusting, but clinging. Mealtimes were clearly an ordeal. He approached the table with the utmost wariness yet he seemed so hungry. The first mouthful or two would go down, then he would stiffen, turn white, begin to choke, and up it would all come. He sat staring at his plate of defiled food with a mixture of revulsion and fear, though the fear seemed related to what had come out of him rather than what would happen to him.

On the evidence of the first day it seemed likely that the fear of being sick and the sickness itself were distressing him more than any other aspect of mealtimes; it also seemed as though immediate action might be kinder than waiting to see what would happen for he was in such distress of mind.

The nursery was in an old Georgian house with high panelled rooms and big open fireplaces, and the children's dining-room was only used at mealtimes. The next day I told Tony that we would have our dinner together when the other children were having their rest, so he just sat quietly on my lap in the armchair by the fire while the other children served each other beautifully and we looked on approvingly. How incredible children are in times of need! Their concern for Tony and their faith that he would soon be better must have reached and warmed him.

When we were alone by the fire I explained what we were going to do. Being sick didn't matter a bit but it smelled horrid, it looked horrid and it tasted horrid, so we would just make sure that none of those things spoilt his dinner. I fetched a white pail of warm water with a lid and put it on one side of the armchair, then we put a few drops of Dettol in it and he sniffed to see if he liked it and he did. Then half a dozen pretty plates and spoons were put on a low table on the other side of the chair, together with three dishes of food with lids and tea-cosies to keep them hot, and several clean mugs and a jug of water. Then I took him on my lap again and explained once more, very slowly.

We would put a small dinner on a small plate and he could eat some, and he might finish it all up and want some more, and we might not want the pail at all. But if he was sick it wouldn't matter a bit because we would just drop the plate and the dinner and the sick into the pail and put the lid on! He liked that and smiled.

So we started, very cautiously, and the first dinner-plate was quietly disposed of a few moments later. We waited a bit, had a drink of water, and then he said 'More', so we tried again. We nearly made it that time, but not quite, so the second dinner-plate quietly followed the first and a pleasant whiff of Dettol came up between removing the lid and replacing it.

Tony contemplated everything quietly for several minutes, then said 'More'. He finished the next small helping, took a cautious breath or two, waited a minute or two, then holding the plate out said 'More, a big one', and he ate it all with unhurried enjoyment. Then he put the plate on the table, took off his bib, climbed back on to my lap, put his thumb in his mouth and went to sleep. He woke as the others came down for tea, got off my lap to join them, and never looked back.

A great ally was George, who had the appetite of a horse.

Reluctant eaters would be put next to George and when their food was put in front of them and they said 'I don't want any' it was safe to say kindly: 'Well I'll leave it there just in case you change your mind, but it doesn't matter if you don't want it – George can have it when he's finished his'. This gave the child two or three minutes to decide whether or not to try it, and George always said very nicely 'Now can I have yours?' and waited for the nod of assent before making very short work of his second dinner. After a few days the message went home, and the reluctant eater would guard his portion with one arm whilst spooning his food in with his other, and at that point all that remained to be said was: 'It's all right, there is no hurry, George can have some more from the big dish if he is still hungry.'

Dear George, he helped so many children. But what isn't helpful is for an adult to say artificially 'If you don't eat it up, I'll have it!' It is bad practice to threaten if the threat isn't carried out, and surely no one should eat any-one else's food after it has been *given* to them without the courtesy of asking and receiving permission? If the meal is not wanted, then it can legitimately be eaten, or given to the cat, or put into the stock-pot, but no useful purpose is served by putting it before the child at the next meal for that adds to the problem by turning it into a trial of strength.

Elizabeth taught me a lesson about the fear of eating unknown food in strange places. Elizabeth was one of thirteen children, and she was so hungry that she dribbled as the smell of food met her outside the dining room, but once seated she would hang her head, flush scarlet, sit stiffly in her chair and refuse to eat. I thought she might feel hemmed in and moved her to the top of the table but it didn't help. She was invited to serve the dinner, to carry the plates, and to eat with me before or after the others ate, but nothing worked.

Then it dawned on me that chips might be a more familiar dinner, so next day I went out and bought some. She jumped to her feet, eyes shining, and threw herself at me laughing in anticipation as I entered the dining room with the familiar parcel. I told her to sit down while

157

I put it on the plate, but as it was put in front of her she went stiff again, hung her head and wept. Suddenly I understood, and tipped it all back into the paper and handed it to her. She snatched it and rushed out of the room, and following her at a discreet distance I found her sitting on the bottom step of the stairs wolfing the food between sobs.

For days the pattern was repeated, and then one day she brought her parcel to eat at one of the little tables with the others. The next day she allowed a plate to be put under the parcel, and the day after sat quietly as a bit of the paper at each side of the plate was torn off to keep it out of her neighbours' dinner; next day she trimmed the paper herself, smaller still, and so it continued until eventually she had her dinner on a plate with a newspaper doily. Then she began to share her chips with the others, and they shared their dinner with her, and fingers and tablecloths grew incredibly messy but it seemed a small price to pay for helping a child to feel at home.

You may well have noticed your own child bend his head to sniff cautiously if unfamiliar food is put before him. Think twice before saying 'Don't do that, it's rude', for it is a perfectly natural primitive instinct and one that still stands us all in good stead. Don't we all sniff food to make sure that it hasn't gone off, and sniff puddings and stews to judge whether we have added enough spice or herbs? And many of us will remember the sharp aroma of pickles or marmalade cooking when we came in from school, and the effect it had on our salivary glands.

Always let a child sniff an unknown dish, or even a familiar one if it is being eaten in strange surroundings, and if a hostess raises her eyebrows and says 'He's *sniffing* it!' back your child and say staunchly, 'No wonder, it smells delicious, and I wish I was young enough to pay you the same compliment.'

Poor appetites during convalescence can be worrying and this was where I lost my own confidence. Our five-year-old had been very ill indeed with measles and after four weeks in bed, and endless broken nights for all of us, the whole family was at a very low ebb. Water, small drinks of orange juice and smaller ones of milk, a few peeled grapes and postage stamps of bread and butter didn't seem the way back to health and strength. Steamed fish, scrambled eggs, soup, jelly, egg custard and cereals were either ignored or tasted listlessly before being pushed away. Pretty plates and dishes, festive disposable waxed cartons and the doll's tea service didn't have any effect. I even tried stewed apple and ice-cream in a cut-glass salt-cellar with the salt spoon.

There came a Saturday morning when my husband was at work and I was so tired and anxious that it felt as though I had two kilos of lead in each shoe and cotton wool in my head. I couldn't think of anything else to do. Her eight-year-old brother asked if he could have his pocket money and go shopping, so off he went and I went up to read to Mandy yet again until she dozed off, leaving me free to try to catch up with the jobs downstairs.

I didn't hear Simon come in, but suddenly I was aware of gales of real hearty laughter coming from both children upstairs; it seemed weeks since I heard anything so lovely and I ran up with winged heels to see what was happening. Mandy was sitting up in bed full of beans and looking radiant. Simon was sitting at the end of the bed, and they were playing ball with screwed up sheets of newspaper reeking of chips. With real joy and pride Simon said, 'I spent all my money on chips, and she's eaten the lot!' A little of what you fancy does you good!

Later Mandy taught me about drinking after having her tonsils out. She announced one morning: 'If I sip little sips it hurts every time, but if I swallow in big long swallows that don't stop, it doesn't hurt at all.' I once mentioned this to a nurse, and she said 'But of course!' as if this were a matter of common knowledge. However, I pass this piece of information on, since I suspect it is not as widely known as she thinks.

Some food likes and dislikes have to be accepted. Strong or distinctive flavours such as ginger biscuits, salad cream, vinegar, sauces, pickles and oxtail soup tend to be loved or loathed. The texture of some foods may also attract or repel, and to this day tripe, the skin on boiled milk and the crinkly leaves of a savoy cabbage are three things that I dislike to feel in my mouth – rhubarb, too, which puts my teeth on edge.

Other foods have unfortunate associations. The last thing eaten before being sick may put us off that particular thing for quite a time even though it may not have been responsible for the sickness. Some children hate sweet foods, and this is all to the good although it poses certain problems as I discovered when a hostess told me with affectionate delight (fortunately) that our four-year-old had shaken her hand at the end of a party and said, 'Mummy says I am to thank you. I can't thank you for the tea because I didn't like it. But it was very kind of you to ask me.'

It seems that the Marmite sandwiches and sausages on sticks were in short supply, and Simon's dislike of sweet things was such that he couldn't eat the scones, biscuits, jellies, cakes and trifles. Thereafter he had two rounds of his favourite scrambled-egg sandwiches before he set off for any party, and there was no further cause for honesty that might have met with a less sympathetic response elsewhere.

If children are becoming fussy beyond the bounds of genuine dislike, for example nibbling the butter and sultanas out of a scone and leaving the rest, then it is reasonable to meet the request for another scone with 'No more, you are full up already.' But if he continues to beg and you know that he isn't full, and can sense that he was experimenting with the scone out of interest but has now put himself in a difficult position from which he can't extricate himself, it sometimes pays to help him to save face. On such an occasion (but *not* regularly) it can ease the situation to say, 'I'll tell you what, just sometimes it helps to make room if you walk once round the table standing very tall, try it.' When he returns to a confident 'Now see if there is room for those pieces', there usually is, plus another scone eaten up completely.

Children are quick to know the difference between a weak parent and a strong parent who is confident enough to make a magnanimous gesture to save them from losing face.

One last point is worth bearing in mind. Each family knows the times of day when their particular children need sleep, and the times of the day when their appetites are heartiest. The patterns vary from child to child. Some children have two naps in the day and sleep all night until they are three, some give up daytime sleeping within the first six months, and the individual variations even within the same family are very wide indeed. Similarly some children eat three good meals a day whilst others eat only one good meal, and it may be breakfast, dinner or tea.

You may feel that your child doesn't like dinners, but the bacon, egg, fish, liver, meat or sausage that he doesn't want in the middle of the day may be eaten with relish at breakfast or tea time. Whether or not you can cook them at these times is another matter, but the first thing to do is to discover whether it is the food or the time of day that causes you to think that he doesn't like dinners.

If it is the time of day, then his main meal needs to be planned carefully so that it is well balanced and not just a filling-up with cereal or bread and butter and cake. It is more usual for the midday meal to be the main one, but there may come a time when the morning nap is outgrown but by lunch time he is too tired to eat much, and then a heavy sleep leaves him refreshed for a large tea but unready for bed.

If this is the pattern while he is adjusting his sleep needs, then go along with it for a while, or try a light lunch half an hour earlier so that the afternoon nap is shorter and less heavy; or try a substantial breakfast to give him the energy to last out until a light early lunch without becoming tired and cross.

This change-over phase doesn't usually last very long, and important as routine is it pays to be flexible during this period and to recognise the connection between sleep patterns and eating patterns.

Going Out

Toddlers need fresh air and exercise every day and so do their parents. The trouble is that those who need it most so often find it most difficult to organise.

Mothers shut up with their children in blocks of flats have special needs and special difficulties. A survey was carried out on the inhabitants of a block of high-rise flats and one of the findings was that every interviewer spontaneously commented to the project leader on the peace and quiet of the higher flats. Yet when the questionnaires were analysed and it was found that the complaint that headed the list was 'my nerves' and one of the most frequently blamed causes given by the top-flat dwellers was 'the noise': it seemed that taut nerves react to every dripping tap, chiming clock, banging door, to noisy neighbours and to the wind.

Flat dwellers in other areas tell of their feeling of perpetual exhaustion. They know it would be sensible to get the children out but can't face the thought of lifts that don't work (some dare not use lifts alone for fear of 'something going wrong') or flights of stairs to negotiate with children and prams. One mother put it succinctly: 'You just can't cope, so you stay in and shout at them or watch the telly.'

Dwellers in more pleasant blocks of flats still talk about this feeling of inertia. One mother made a point of going down to the communal green each day only to find that her child screamed with fear as the lorries thundered by. From the flat window seven floors up they had looked like dinky toys moving smoothly along ribbon roads to the accompaniment of a pleasant background murmur. At first the child just wanted to hold hands and watch from the safety of the entrance, then she moved nearer to the railings bordering the pavement, then finally she turned her back on the traffic and they started to play with balls and push-and-pull toys, and invented jumping and stepping-stone games.

Soon other mothers saw what was going on and sent their own children down to join her. At first she was fed up and resentful but after buying a small folding chair she thoroughly enjoyed sitting and watching them all as they played together. Their greatest joy was simply to run and shout to their hearts' content, and to push each other. This sensitively watching mother said: 'It was hardly ever unkind, it was almost as though it was their way of shaking hands and saying "How do you do, I'm me, who are you?" They explored each other with surprise and delight.'

Children need to let go and to feel free, and it is difficult to feel free unless you can run until you are out of breath without reaching a limiting boundary, and to shout all you want to shout after constantly being told to be quiet. They also need to see the sky above them, to feel grass beneath them and the sun, wind and even rain on their faces, and to meet other children in a space big enough to prevent the anxious feeling that comes to us all if we are crowded too closely before we have had a chance to size things up from a distance.

Many mothers have discovered what a transformation a small stool or chair makes to a visit to the park, beach, village green or even a churchyard if that is the only outdoor space available. As one put it: 'If you are standing around you are always saying "Come on", but if you can sit comfortably out of the wind it's very pleasant just to turn off and watch them potter about.'

Some determined town mothers have their children in the parks soon after eight in the morning during the lighter months of the year because they feel the air is fresher then. The tenacity with which parents will strive to do what is best for their children under the most adverse conditions is often unacknowledged or underrated. In the winter time when it is wet or bitterly cold many gather in undercover shopping precincts or go into the big stores and wander around 'just to get out really, you'd go barmy if you stayed indoors alone all day'.

Going out falls into two main categories for adults: going out for a change of scene as much as for fresh air and exercise, and going out for a definite purpose, such as shopping.

The toddler makes no such distinction, for him all going out is a lovely change, with things to see and hear and touch and smell and do. Outings would be so very much easier if toddlers understood the difference between a work outing and a pleasure outing, but they don't, and wise parents know instinctively that there has to be a compromise. One such moment of compromise arises when an insistent voice says 'Out! Out!' just as parents, pushchair and purchases are heading for home with brisk efficiency.

On bad days most parents know the ensuing dialogue only too well: 'We'll soon be home now and you can push it the last little bit.' 'Out! Out!' 'Can you see that big dog over there? I wonder what he had for dinner?' 'Out! Out!' 'Let's just get over the next road.' 'Out! Out!' 'And when we get to the big red pillar box you can push it.' 'Out! Out!' 'Now stop it.' 'Out!' '*Stop it!*' . . . 'OUT NOW!'

Parents grit their teeth and push on regardless, ignoring the passers-by who have balloons coming out of their heads signifying 'poor little soul', or 'poor woman', or 'poor man', according to their point of identification as they survey the screaming child and exasperated pusher.

On good days parents can be patient and understanding as they unstrap him, lift him out and prepare to guide the pushchair as he staunchly clutches the handle and staggers off. There are several variations on this theme, all familiar and positively endearing on good days. He may be very happy to walk between you and the push-

165

chair, holding the handles at his shoulder level; progress is slow but steady and it is surprising how far his small legs will carry him. He may decline your help very firmly, which offers two alternatives: he may reach up with the clear intention of pushing as you push in which case the pushchair tips over under his weight, or he may push holding lower down in which case the vehicle becomes his battering ram.

Steering something with four wheels is an art that he hasn't yet acquired and the slight change of pressure that alters the direction wildly is as surprising to him as it is alarming to you. He puffs and pants, tugs and pushes, and scores a lamp-post, a shopping trolley and several unsuspecting pairs of legs, while you alternately apologise and make a judicious grab to avoid the next collision. As you watch his erratic progress you will come to understand the nature of his difficulty and then it is easier to see that he needs to practise the art of pushing and steering in the garden, in the park or along the flat landing before combining it with a shopping outing.

Running, stumbling and bumbling along with an empty pushchair in a large space is fun and good exercise, but learning to control its direction needs more time and thought. He can try to push it round you as you sit, or round a tree or a flower-bed, or along a path. Or you can play at pretending the pushchair is your dog by tying a piece of string on the front and then walking ahead saying 'Would you and your dog like to come for a walk with me?' As his steering ability improves you can change your walking pattern from a straight line to a curve, then a corner, then a zigzag.

You can congratulate yourself if you can find play ways of helping your toddler to learn this difficult new skill, and then patiently let him push the pram for part of each subsequent outing. You can also congratulate yourself if you know that just sometimes he has to be pushed whether he likes it or not.

Each day's outing will give the maximum benefit if it combines three important elements. First is an opportunity to run and jump and climb until he is out of breath. This doesn't mean that he has to be chased until he is distressed or exhausted, but just that a little extra effort will cause him to breathe deeply and expand his lungs, improve his circulation and strengthen his muscles.

The second element is to encounter new experiences to stimulate his curiosity, and have time to satisfy that curiosity – not just to see you post a letter but to be lifted up to drop the letter in himself; not just to see the ducks on the pond but to throw them stale bread that you have taken with you; not just to walk along the path, but to step on and off the kerb repeatedly (where it is practical to do so, for negotiating a kerb safely is part of learning to cross a road).

The third element is a period of tranquillity.

The rhythm of being pushed is a delight in its own right and it would be as sad to keep up a ceaseless flow of chatter and stimulation as it would be to maintain an apathetic silence. So go out for all the reasons associated with health, and for practical reasons, and for sociable ones, but don't overlook the need we all have to be at peace with ourselves, each other, and the world that is all about us.

Bedtime

At the end of a long and demanding day most parents long for their toddler's bedtime even if they dread the bit between the announcement and the goodnight kiss. The best of parents become all too human by the evening and tired toddlers can become tyrants.

After a lovely day the toddler doesn't want bed to bring it to an end, and strenuously says 'No, no' as he puts as much distance between himself and you as possible. Retrieving him from under the table is difficult, especially if you are pregnant. After a fractious day bed is the final battleground and it is difficult to see why he isn't as anxious as you are to bring it all to a swift conclusion in the hope of a better day tomorrow. After a day when nothing has held his attention for very long he invariably finds something of totally absorbing interest in the last ten minutes, and wild horses won't drag him away.

But just occasionally everything goes right and a compliant child is carried off to the bathroom just for the shared pleasure of being held close. The bath or wash is accompanied by contented murmurings and cooperative limbs. Clean, warm and cherubic in night attire, he nestles in loving arms on the journey to bed, and the lashes flicker down in sleep almost before the last kiss and tucking-in.

Parents all have their own ideas on what constitutes bedtime, but few would have either the stamina or the inclination to emulate one couple who said of their three-year-old almost proudly, 'We're all dead tired, Pumpkin didn't want to go to bed until three o'clock this morning.' Bedtime should be your decision, for your child's security is rooted in the knowledge that you are able to control the main events of each day with predictability. Your toddler can remember and respond to the sequence of events better than to clock-time, though that too is acquired with habit eventually.

The practical significance of this is that bed at six o'clock (or whatever) is better as an aim for *you* than for him, and bed at *about* six o'clock is more likely to allow you to tuck him up finally at the time of your choice. In short, it is better to aim at the in-bed time rather than the going-to-bed time.

Even the best of parents can become disorganised by the end of a day: the unexpected happens; there are delays in shops and buses; some meals involve longer preparation and clearing up; extra jobs have to be fitted in. Whatever the reason, the run-up to bedtime becomes rushed, and with one eye on the clock you reckon that you can just about get him into bed before Dad comes in for his meal, or older children have to be taken somewhere, or your favourite TV programme begins. But that is reckoning on his being a willing accomplice, and since he is a person in his own right he can't possibly be passive every time you become disorganised any more than his proper readiness time can always match your highly organised clock-time. Try to assess the situation at least half an hour before bedtime.

Think of your own link with the clock. If you have ten minutes in hand for a five-minute walk to the station you can enjoy the walk; if you have seven minutes tension begins to mount; if you have six minutes anxiety quickens your pulse as well as your step; and if you fear you are late then exasperation and frustration add to the turmoil. Your toddler reacts in much the same way.

The natural rounding-off of whatever he is doing may only be ten minutes away, but if he is interrupted suddenly with the call 'Bedtime, come along. Put that away – quickly' there is an instinctive arousal of strong feelings which, if he could put them into words, might be expressed like this: 'No, no . . . careful . . . I've just put that there specially . . . you don't understand . . . you're spoiling it all . . . I shan't be a minute . . . please stop and listen . . . but I can't explain in words . . . and I'm getting panicky because I can't explain . . . and you're not looking or listening . . . and now it's all too late . . . *I hate you.*' The tears and the tantrum express what he couldn't find words to say, and then it takes so much out of you both from then on – and far longer in time to heal than the ten minutes that he needed originally.

Always give a child at least ten minutes warning before you want him to stop what he is doing, even if you can't see that he is doing anything in particular. His imagination may be wandering far away and he needs time to come back to everyday reality, time to tune into you again. If he is clearly involved in something important then it helps if you can enter into the spirit of his play. 'When you've finished that castle shall we leave it for Daddy to see?' is more friendly than 'Put your bricks away', but you must honour the suggestion if he agrees. If he is sorting objects with a system all his own then sit beside him and watch and learn; if his concentration should hold for five or ten minutes then that experience plus a wash is more valuable than a cutting short of the experience for a bath.

Enjoy his enjoyment and refrain from the routine clearing up if you sense that he treasures what he has done. If you are there at the beginning of the activity and can see what is likely to happen you can offer a tray saying, 'Would you like to put them all on this tray? then we won't have to tidy up when you have finished.' At the end of the play he may well go to bed with alacrity if you ask him whether he would like the tray put by his bed – and then the play can be revived when he sees it the next morning, which is an added bonus for both of you.

If he suddenly realises that something precious has been left outside, you misunderstand his feelings if you say, 'It doesn't matter, it will be quite all right.' What he is trying to convey is that he identifies with the object so

170

strongly that to leave it outside is like feeling himself to be outside, and he can't possibly face the thought of himself being left out in the dark and cold all night. Go with him, and be patient as he brings his imaginary other self safely inside in the shape of a little car, a new spade or even a special stone. If he wants to put something to bed in a box, pram or chair, understand that at the moment 'it' is a small but real person and he doesn't want this poor person to be left in an uncomfortable and chilly state all night.

Children's imaginations are very strong indeed, and fantasy and reality become confused quite naturally at this stage. If you say in effect 'You don't have to bother about that person being alone and frightened outside, or cold and uncomfortable inside', you are going directly against your teaching of kindness and consideration to others.

If the day has been difficult for both of you then a full hour before bedtime it may not come amiss to say, 'Let's go and have a lovely long play in the bath!' The idea of a play in the bath is quite different from the idea of early bed, but you must genuinely see this as a play period and not an early night in disguise. Some of you may literally bath with your child; some may use the friendly plural to indicate that you will both be enjoying it even though he is in the bath and you are sitting peacefully alongside.

As long as you top up with hot water at intervals and don't leave him alone, there is no reason why he shouldn't spend half an hour or more in the bath. If you habitually soak for hours as your way of unwinding you will understand how soothing immersion in warm water can be. Sometimes children become so immersed in their play that they forget the slipperiness of the bath, and in reaching or turning quickly they may be completely submerged and frightened. A rubber bath mat with suction pads to anchor it firmly in place may restore confidence. But for other children the slippery bottom is one of their

171

great enjoyments as they swish up and down.

Your toddler may enjoy a long play with a small metal teapot, for the spout of water tickles a bare tummy and knees and back in a very particular way that is more long-lasting than the trickles from a flannel or the splosh from a yogurt pot. Or he may enjoy floating toys, and the fun of pushing them to the bottom of the bath and watching them leap to the surface. Or he may enjoy watching you wash your hands very slowly and very thoroughly, and then trying to copy your movements with his own small fingers which haven't yet learned to do such complicated twistings and turnings (a bath is a good place to practise new skills such as hand-washing for there is ample time and no fear of spills and wet sleeves).

Towards the end of the play time he may love the game of 'Which bit shall we wash first? and which next?' You probably have an ordered sequence of washing, and when you say 'Now one hand . . . now the other hand . . . now a leg' his response will be from habit as much as the recognition of the name of each part of his anatomy. It is a challenge if you ask him to name which part he wants you to wash, and he may think hard and then thrust a hand out silently but with eyes a-sparkle – he may need to enjoy the choice silently to begin with, it takes time to choose-and-say together.

During long and peaceful baths there is time to prolong the pleasure of both the washing and being together by the occasional running commentary: 'Let's wash your face, first your nose . . . now one cheek, now the other . . . now one eyebrow, now the other . . . now your chin . . . and your forehead . . . now shut one eye, now the other.' The shared pleasure in each other is what matters most, for the knowledge that grows slowly but surely through these genuine play experiences is largely dependent upon the bond between you.

If there is a vehement reaction to the suggestion that it is time to get out of the bath try 'All right, you can stay until the water has all gone.' Almost certainly when the moment comes for the last of the water to gurgle dramatically down the plughole there will be a frantic call of 'Take me out, take me out, I shall go down the hole' and you will be the kind rescuer instead of the villain of the piece. But if he continues to resist, then the time has come to lift him out bodily and wrap him in a large towel. Resistance is difficult to keep up within a towel and the warmth and rubbing and a continuous murmur of chat usually restore calmness quite quickly.

Often Dad returns from work while the bath is still in progress, and since this may be the only time of the day when he sees his child awake he may want to share the bathing or to take it over completely. Sometimes this generates such excitement that it ends in tears; sometimes the presence of two parents represents too strong a disciplinary force and a tantrum is sparked off; sometimes the toddler refuses to get out of the bath or into bed and enjoys the sense of power involved in playing one parent off against the other; sometimes Dad can cope more easily than the mother who has been with him all day and she gratefully leaves the two together and goes downstairs to finish cooking until it is time for the goodnight kiss; sometimes one parent completes the bathing while the other sits quietly reading a bedtime story, and this can induce a delightful feeling of peace and unity at the end of a busy day.

It may take time to find the pattern that suits you all best, but mothers should think very carefully before saying 'Please don't come up until he's in bed, you'll only excite him.' If fathers are shut out in these early years mothers will undoubtedly regret it later, and may not even trace the connection as they say 'Why is it always me who has to look after him at weekends? You just don't seem to be interested in him.' It is difficult to feel involved and responsible if you are shut out of the relationship early on, or made to feel inadequate.

In theory, once children are tucked up in bed and kissed goodnight (never ever withold the goodnight kiss for this is the talisman that keeps them safe during the hours of darkness and the mystery of sleep), then they sleep peacefully until the morning. But you will be an exceptionally rare family if you can take this for granted, and most of us know several variations on this theme.

There is the child who goes to sleep immediately, only to wake up before dawn refreshed and raring to start a new day. At best you will hear singing, talking and games going on that involve a lot of banging and thumping. At worst you will be brightly invaded, clambered over and softened up with snuggles and kisses before the hopeful suggestion 'Shall I read you a story? I got a book.' In between comes the semi-sleeping state as you dimly become aware of the background noises, followed by sudden silence which wakes you in a flash – 'What's he up to? Has he gone downstairs? If so, what's he doing?' Naturally you have to go and investigate, without pausing for slippers or dressing-gown, only to find that miraculously he has gone to sleep again on the floor wrapped in his cuddly blanket. You carefully cover him with one more layer and return to bed, frozen, wide awake and unable to take advantage of the respite he has offered.

Then there is the child who just doesn't go to sleep or even stay in bed. You listen to the thump of tiny feet and either turn a deaf ear or call out, 'Get back into bed!' There is usually silence for a bit and then it starts again, so up you go to try to induce a sleepy state by being very kind and patient as you put him to bed for the second time. After the third or fourth trip upstairs patience wears thin, but he pretends not to notice as he calls down after you 'When you come up to smack me can I have a drink of water?'

Once I spent the evening with the mother of one of these children, and we worked out together what we would do if and when he came downstairs to join the two of us as we sat by the fire. We decided that we would simply carry on as though he wasn't there unless intervention was necessary for his safety. This joint plan removed any embarrassment between us, and we quite looked forward to playing the game to see if it would work. We were having coffee from a tray on a low table by the fire when her two-year-old erupted into the room and took up his stance in the doorway with a magnificent stage presence. He stood his ground with a dazzling smile and we continued our conversation with no indication that we had noticed his entrance. He was momentarily taken aback to find that his performance had fallen so flat, but trotted off to an armchair and clambered into it importantly. His mother, carefully looking at me as she continued to talk, crossed the room to shut the door and came back to resume her seat. He began to play, trying to catch our attention at first by putting cushions on his head and generally showing off. We continued to talk quite genuinely since we were enjoying each other.

Then he really played, walking between us to fetch the hearth set of poker, brush and tongs (we were at the ready in case he stumbled and fell into the fire, but he never knew it) and taking it to the centre of the room where he hooked and unhooked each piece from the stand several times. Then he fetched shawls and scarves from the dressing-up box and enveloped both himself and them. The game over he looked at us both again, and then at the two biscuits on the plate by the coffee-pot. With one accord we stretched out our hands and took one each. That was a distinct disappointment, and he got his own back by going to the piano and banging with both hands. We let him get on with it for a bit and then his mother serenely walked over, removed his hands safely from the keyboard, and shut the lid. Miraculously it stayed shut. Perhaps he was losing confidence in his ability to make himself the centre of attention and didn't want to risk another failure. He climbed on to various chairs, looked at books, sucked his thumb, and began to lose the energy that had been sparked into life by the excitement of his plan to disrupt the evening peace yet again.

Finally a somewhat deflated and rather chilly little boy opened the door and disappeared. It was tempting to do all the maternal things like take him a hot-water bottle and tuck him up warmly, but we both felt that this would give him the satisfaction of knowing that he had penetrated our consciousness after all, so we didn't. But about ten minutes later his mother went upstairs and looked in as though on her routine late night check-up, and reported that he was fast asleep.

We had an advantage in that I was only a friend, and it was easier for the mother and me to break the established pattern together than it might have been for the mother and father. But if you decide to try it for yourselves you can still plan together beforehand and carry it through, relying on each other to keep all emotion at bay and to maintain a convincing and natural conversational tone and content.

When the children are older the reversal of this game is often effective. They come downstairs saying that they aren't tired, so the parents say 'Well, we are, so we'll go up now and have an early night – will you turn the lights out when you're ready to come up?' This often results in a scurry to get into bed, partly in order not to be left downstairs alone, but partly in order not to miss the goodnight kiss and tucking in.

Another habit can start with a genuine nightmare – and don't imagine that children can't have such things. You may be able to remember back to your own childhood and the real terror that woke you up sometimes, and when it happens there is only one possible thing to do – get into the warm parental bed as quickly as possible and feel the protection of their close proximity.

This may be repeated for several nights or weeks if the nightmares have been sparked off by some distressing incident, for the original memory can't fade before the child has recovered from whatever it was. In our case it was a road accident that we came upon while one car was still in flames and the fire engine and ambulance were still there. Our seven-year-old was unperturbed, but the four-year-old was terrified of fire for a long while afterwards, and even with the extinction of our coal fire at her bedtime, and the ladder on the lawn 'in case', she still came into our bed at some point during the night for weeks. When this happens it usually results in a general post: the child comes in, clambers over the nearest one and snuggles down safely in the middle, to be followed eventually by father or mother departing for the child's bed. At least everyone gets their sleep that way.

The coming of summer often solves the problem, especially if the curtains are opened after the child has gone to sleep for dawn comes early and fears flee before daylight. Or sometimes the light bulb can be changed for one of the very small glimmering red ones that can be left on all night; or a 'lion' pyjama case can be given as a special present 'to look after you all night'; or the position of the furniture in the child's bedroom can be changed, for often a habit can be broken by changing as much as possible of the related background. In this case, bedtime and sleeping has acquired its own fears, so try changing the environment of going to bed.

But none of these things is likely to work if you cut short the period of comfort. It is only when it looks as though the comfort itself is becoming a habit that it is appropriate to try to release the child from that pattern by offering another one.

Talking to Your Toddler

Most of us have probably said to our older children more than once 'Why don't you listen? I've told you again and again', and I don't suppose I am the only one who has been told by exasperated children 'You've put on your listening face but you *aren't* listening.'

Parents are constantly being told now of the importance of language in the intellectual development of their children, but an overemphasis on language can do as much harm as good if we don't first know where we stand on the even more important issue of communication.

During my years in a child guidance clinic it wasn't uncommon to ask the parents of backward talkers how much they spoke to their child, and for their answer to be an incredulous 'Talk to him? But he's only four, he wouldn't understand.' They genuinely thought that talking was something that just 'happened' naturally when the child was ready, like cutting teeth and learning to walk. Fortunately, although verbal communication had been minimal the unspoken communication of 'I love you, I'll look after you, and I'll keep you safe no matter what happens' had often come through loud and clear, and since the child was emotionally secure and the parents tended to be confident people (if limited in their understanding) it wasn't long before they were learning to talk to each other.

Other parents would say, 'Talk to her? But whatever would I say? I'd feel so daft.' This was a more difficult problem. Often the sense of inadequacy and self-consciousness was so deeply seated that these parents had withdrawn into themselves in such a way that the child couldn't even receive the message that he was loved and secure. Confidence and speech needed reinforcement on both sides. This took longer but was deeply rewarding because each responded to the other with such relief and happiness once the barriers were down.

Although some children suffered from speech defects, and others were late starters for a variety of reasons, a great many children were held back simply because their parents had had no contact with young children before giving birth to their own and therefore they knew nothing at first hand about the early stages of development, especially about the need to talk.

A great many parents who 'know nothing about babies' discover that lurking in their memories there is in fact a deep well of forgotten experience to draw on, and for them a great deal 'comes naturally'. Others may not have such happy memories, or they may be blocked by anxiety. Others are habitually silent people, like the mother who said 'I'm just a comfortable cabbage!' or the one who said 'I live inside myself a lot, thinking and day-dreaming.' For their own sakes as well as their children's, silent parents should try to make the effort to talk with their children, and to other people, for internal and external dialogue need to balance each other if we are to go on growing and developing.

Parents *do* need to know how much personal contact through speech means to their children emotionally, and how dependent on words they are going to be for their intellectual growth, but sometimes knowing what is necessary is not enough and there is a real need to see and hear how it can be done.

Copying plays an important part in learning at every stage, and I remember this being demonstrated by a Sister in the maternity hospital where our first child was born. The young mother in the bed next to mine was very apprehensive and didn't know what to make of it when a cheerful young nurse handed her baby over saying 'Go on, go to your mum for a feed and a chat!' The mother had as much as she could manage to overcome her shyness and anxiety about breast-feeding, and was near to tears as she said, 'What did she mean about a feed and a chat?'

At the next feed it was the Sister who carried her baby to her, chatting all the while in a comforting monologue: 'Now don't be impatient . . . I'm being as quick as I can . . . and there's your mother looking as pretty as a picture. Now just you be careful of her even if you are starving, those breasts of hers are going to be tender for a day or two.'

Over the next few days we all acquired a great deal of information through this chatting (the nurses tried hard to copy but Sister was in a class of her own), and in addition we were all talking to our babies naturally and easily. On the day we left, her last words were: 'Go on talking to your baby and soon he'll try to talk back in his own way. You can start to be friends long before he can talk to you properly.' If we all aimed at establishing friendship through speech we wouldn't go far wrong.

Some parents talk incessantly, and if the quantity of talk was a measure of children's intellectual development then all their offspring would be genii. But voluble talkers are not always successful either in forming bonds of friendship or in helping a child to learn what is in effect a foreign language. In the nicest possible way and without even realising it, it is very easy to issue a stream of orders from morning until night: 'Time to get up . . . into the bathroom, quickly . . . breakfast's ready, sit up . . . finish your crust . . . clean your teeth . . . go and play . . . get your coat, hurry up . . . hold my hand . . . no, don't touch . . . look where you're going . . . give me your coat . . . wash your hands for dinner, quickly . . . no, you can't get down yet . . . hurry up and finish it . . . run and play . . . tea time . . . put your toys away . . . quickly . . . upstairs . . . shut your eyes so the soap doesn't get in . . . out you come . . . clean your teeth . . . into bed . . . now go to sleep quickly.'

On and on we go, and it's hurry, hurry, hurry all the way.

A child can learn to respond like a puppet, without thought or question, and always in a subordinate relationship rather than in friendship. He doesn't even need to learn to speak the language as long as he can understand and respond appropriately.

Requests are more courteous than orders (though for safety's sake children must learn to respond immediately to orders should they be necessary), but a question is often best of all because of its implied friendship: 'We shall be going for a walk in a minute, what shall we both put on?' This calls for thought and discussion – coats? mackintoshes? cardigans? scarves? hats? gumboots? If enough time is allowed all this learning can come about quite naturally – sometimes in a spirit of earnest consideration, sometimes in fun – and with luck and good management the words 'quickly' and 'hurry up' needn't be used at all.

Another form of monologue comes from the parent who is relieving his or her own feelings – 'No, don't do that, I've only just separated all the screws from the nails. Now you've mixed them up again. What did you want to go and do that for? I don't know, as fast as I do one job you undo it. It's all very well for you, you aren't the one who has to mend things when they get broken, and half the time if it wasn't for you they wouldn't get broken in the first place.'

Parents are only human and we all need to relieve our feelings from time to time, but we need to check up on ourselves lest it becomes a habit – for if it does our children are very likely to pick it up since they are exposed to it all day and every day. And then we moan at them for moaning!

One mother said, 'My husband came in one evening and I started to talk when he suddenly said in a dark brown voice "Don't drip all over me the minute I come in." It pulled me up and I was grateful because I hadn't realised until then that I'd got into this awful habit of moaning.'

181

Another habit of speech that many will recognise even if we don't use it ourselves is an incessant flow of bright but superficial chatter. My great aunt was adept at this, as my sister and I discovered when she came to look after us once when our mother was in hospital. At first we listened intently in the expectation that she was going to say something genuinely interesting, and then we stopped bothering to listen but continued to watch in fascination because the special voice and facial expressions she reserved for children were unlike anything we had ever seen or heard before. We were too young to understand that she didn't have children of her own, or to appreciate her kindness in volunteering to look after a three- and a five-year-old, so when she sniffed the air one day and said archly 'I can smell kippers, they must be the ones Mummy is having for her dinner!' I said crossly 'Don't be silly, you can't smell her dinner – she's too far away', and the tenuous relationship broke down irretrievably.

Twenty-five years later a similar personality came to spend the day with us when our own children were much the same age and when she had gone our four-year-old said 'I didn't like her.' When asked why he said simply 'She talked with her mouf.' Children know with unerring instinct the difference between words that communicate from the heart and the head and those which 'come from the mouth'. What they can't know is the sadness that often lies behind the artificial chatter, sometimes indicating unfamiliarity with children but sometimes revealing an inability to make real contact with anyone.

Another habit that affects almost all of us is that of negativism. It is so easy to say 'Don't' and so difficult to find a 'Do' to put in its place. Two mothers on a play-group course felt that they didn't use the word 'don't' very often, but everyone agreed to go back to her play-group and count one morning to see just how often the word slipped out. The two mothers came back the following week and one said, 'We counted for each other, and

I didn't believe her when she said I'd clocked up twenty-seven "don'ts" before milk time. But after lunch I listened to myself, and she was right, it just kept happening.'

We found that we associated the word 'don't' with a nagging tone of voice (which we all recognised we used from time to time), but what had surprised us was the number of times we were unaware of using it because it was said in a happy and peaceful context, such as 'Don't brush too hard, the sand will go everywhere.' For weeks we all made a real effort to rephrase such comments positively – 'Brush gently and all the sand will go into the dustpan.'

The fact that the negative approach came naturally while the positive approach was an effort of will shocked us into making a determined effort to be positive. Without exception everyone said that her playgroup's atmosphere was noticeably improved, and felt that it wasn't just due to being positive but to thinking before speaking, and therefore what was said was not just a reflex action but a genuine communication with the child concerned.

It is easier for people to boost each other's good resolutions in a group than it is to struggle against odds at home alone, but some parents found that even on a bad day (some said especially on a bad day) it helped them to keep control of themselves by playing the game of 'I won't say "don't" for the next half an hour.' Their own positive concentration stopped them reacting to the child and quite often things simmered down instead of escalating.

Parents who take a natural delight in talking to their toddlers are luckier than they know, for the chances are that they had parents who enjoyed talking to them. Habits of speech reflect attitudes to living and are catching. If parents are generally friendly and courteous to one another then their children often pick up the habit of cooperation and courtesy. Conversely, if they are sarcastic or shout, or are moody or violent, then some of this inevitably rubs off on the children, too. The toddler who has happy, loving parents, who talk to him naturally as the person he is, is a truly privileged child.

These sensitive parents know when to be peacefully silent, when to croon small nothings to comfort distress, when to speak slowly and distinctly to convey a suggestion or request, when to keep up a running commentary on a job in order to hold interest, when to create a diversion to distract a fractious toddler's attention, when to ask a simple question to stimulate him into thinking, when to use a tone of voice that indicates warm approval or disapproval or fun or surprise or danger, when to say 'No' and mean it, when to draw attention to something beautiful or unusual or funny or interesting (without spoiling the magic moment by a flood of explanations that can come next week, next month or next year), when to count things naturally and when not to turn a happy moment into a maths lesson, and when to name colours naturally and when not to spoil such experiences as touching and smelling a scented red rose by the intrusion of any words at all.

Some parents know all these things with a wisdom as old as the hills. But they also shout and are irritable or even cry occasionally because they are human and have learnt that, although self-control is right and proper up to a certain point, if perfection is the aim it can be damaging to their health and personalities – and a great strain for their children, who feel guilty about expressing their own honest feelings in the face of such perfection.

The parents in need of a boost to their confidence are those who are not familiar with young children and have no one to turn to, but who are so anxious to do what is right that they turn to books, many of which contradict each other. Some authors write with only the child in mind; others are sensitive to the parents' own needs and difficulties. Some encourage parents to 'teach' their children; other explain how children learn anyway in a happy and stimulating relationship and environment. Some try to help parents to emulate skilled professional relationships with children; others know that children don't want 'professional parents', they just want comfortably ordinary ones. Some are so concerned with the intellectual development of children that they omit to explain that the primary function of language is to establish a relationship of love and trust – bricks of intellectual development can't be firmly laid one upon another if the foundation is the shifting sand of emotional insecurity.

Parents need the confidence not to trust experts against their own intuition and experience. Books can be helpful so can talking to health visitors, nursery school teachers and others who work with young children, and to other parents, especially those involved with their own and other people's children in mother and toddler clubs and playgroups. But, above all, watch and listen to other adults talking to young children wherever you go – on buses, in cafés, on the beach, at the clinics, in the shops and in each other's homes. Pay attention particularly to grannies, grandads and great-grandparents, because they have the time to listen and talk with their grandchildren, bound by the natural affinity that draws the young and the old together in a refuge of 'being', quietly removed from the middle generation's bustle of 'doing'.

Look and listen, and then act on the old advice, 'What you see good in others carefully imitate, what you see bad in others carefully shun.' But don't copy slavishly. Pick up the idea and translate it in your own way.

The other invaluable aid to learning is to try to pinpoint how you feel when you are learning from your own experience or are being taught by others, for then you will begin to put yourself in your toddler's place and can learn from him and with him before trying to teach him. I learned to drive very late in life and can still remember the feeling that I would never be able to concentrate simultaneously on what my hands and feet were doing inside the car and on the pedestrians, road signs and traffic outside, whilst being responsible for the coordination that linked the two.

A toddler must feel very much like that as he struggles to manipulate his spoon and pusher or fork, and to find his mouth accurately, and to keep his plate on the table, and to keep his sleeves out of the gravy, and not to spill his water, and not to choke.

At the confusing stage of learning, my driving instructor was particularly helpful and just sat beside me quietly reinforcing the separate bits of learning that were beginning to come together: 'Brake gently . . . clutch out . . . and change down. Good, relax. Take all the time you need, you have as much right to be on the road as anybody else.'

The point at which words undermined my confidence and performance was when they were offered too early in my experience, and at those times words like 'You didn't match your engine speed to your road speed' had absolutely no meaning at all, they just flustered me. So it must be for a toddler when he is trying to master a new skill if his attention is distracted too soon to a later stage of learning for which he isn't yet ready.

He may be struggling to push his arm down a coat sleeve, having very carefully memorised that a hand and arm have to be thrust down a small dark tunnel that is lurking somewhere or other in the bundle that is his coat. Imagine how he might feel if, while he is still at the interesting stage of waiting for his hand to emerge from the other end, you interrupt his concentration to say, 'No, not that arm, you've got it in the wrong sleeve, the coat will be back to front, put it in the other sleeve, here, take it out, that's right, no that's the other arm in the other sleeve, you want the same arm in the other sleeve!'

His bewilderment would be just as great if he was managing to put the right bits of his anatomy into the right holes, by a superbly coordinated feat of memory and skill, and you broke into his concentration with 'What's this called? It's a pocket, can you say "pocket"? And where's the other one? That's one, two pockets. Two sleeves and two pockets. And how many buttons? One, two, three, four lovely round buttons. And what colour are they?' If he could think clearly in words, and dared to express his feelings, he would probably feel like saying 'Oh, leave me alone! Can't you see I'm putting on my coat, and that it's very, very difficult? I don't want a lesson in vocabulary, number, shape and colour. Go away!'

One of the great values of talking to children from birth is that it gives them time to become familiar with words long before they need to use them. Take the word 'sleeve'. You have probably used it hundreds of times, going right back to the first vest and woolly jacket stage as you talked to keep your hungry baby from yelling for his food – 'It's all right, it's coming in a minute. Just let's get this arm into this sleeve. Now this one into this sleeve. Now a nice warm nappy. It's coming, it's coming . . . there, food at last!'

You may even remember the occasion when he picked up the word as though he had just heard it for the very first time. He may have said it after you, or he may suddenly have produced it out of the blue: 'sleeve . . . sleeve . . . sleevesleevesleevesleevesleeve!' He may have laughed as though it was the funniest thing he had ever heard, or he may just have gone on repeating it with quiet satisfaction. It didn't mean anything, it was just a word.

And then suddenly, wham! You help him to put on his coat one day and as his arm goes into the hole he thinks or says 'Sleeve!' and he knows it isn't the hole, it's the bit of the coat that will cover his whole arm when the coat is on.

Numbers are learned in the same slow way, from birth onwards. You have probably counted the stairs sometimes as you carry him up to bed, and counted his fingers and toes as you washed and dried them at bath time. He may learn to say 'one, two, three, four, five' with you, but he may well associate 'one' with his thumbs and big toes and 'five' with his little fingers and little toes for a long time to come.

In a playgroup I once saw the magic moment when a four-year-old's counting knowledge went wham! and became the beginning of number knowledge. He had been able to count for years, and had had his fingers and toes counted since babyhood, but on this particular morning a mother had brought a rabbit into the playgroup and the children were gathered round her lap to stroke it and talk. A child asked how many toes a rabbit had, so the mother found a paw and carefully spread the toes on her hand so that they could count. Suddenly the little boy sat down, took off his shoe and sock, counted his toes eagerly and shouted '*I've* got five toes!' Then he took off his other shoe and sock and counted and said 'and I've got five toes on my other foot!' That was the moment when his previous 'counting' became personal knowledge and from then on he would *know* that he had five toes on each foot; but that particular moment couldn't have come if the previous experience of both toes and counting hadn't been building up in his mind over the months and years.

You may have heard or read something that makes you feel you are supposed to be seizing every opportunity to count things with your child, and to teach him his colours, and to help him to understand the difference between 'big', 'bigger' and 'biggest', and the meaning of such words as 'over', 'under', 'above' and 'below'. Don't panic and think that it all has to be done immediately and in a very short space of time. It doesn't and it can't.

Once you understand the way in which a child builds up physical memories (the 'feel' of arms being inserted into dozens of sleeves of all sorts of shapes, sizes, colours and materials) and words memories (hand, arm, elbow, armhole, sleeve, put, push, down, through), and the slow association of the words with the physical experience, you will find yourself valuing as never before the warm natural flow of talk that introduces him slowly to the words that are relevant to the seeing, touching, hearing, smelling, listening and feelings of both of you.

Listening to Your Toddler

Almost certainly you will already have discovered that you have developed the ability to hear the slightest sound during the night, and no matter how tired you are you will probably be out of bed and on your way to investigate before you are fully awake. You may even check that all is well, get back into bed and go off to sleep again without having become fully conscious at all. Daytime listening operates at this level, too. Various noises alert you to investigate at once, and if it is a cry you will know whether it indicates pain, anger, shock, hunger, tiredness or frustration even before you get there. You will even 'hear' silence and will react just as urgently as to certain noises.

This quality of hearing and response derives from the fiercely primitive protective instinct that is born together with the baby. Although the instinct moderates in most parents as the child learns progressively to look after himself I doubt whether it ever really dies in a parent, and certainly it remains very strong in these early years (unless the odds against the parent are so great that he or she has to turn off in defeat or for self-preservation).

So strongly are parents' listening ears attuned to physical safety that they are sometimes deaf to the child's inarticulate cry for the listening of the heart. Your child needs you to listen to him as you listen to your best friend – with interest, concern, understanding and give and take on both sides – but his language is so very limited and his motives and reactions are so far beyond his own understanding that you will have to develop a capacity for empathy.

Empathy is the rare ability to step outside yourself and into the other person with such accuracy that you experience their feelings as though they were yours, and then to step back inside yourself again so that you can say and do those things that indicate you have heard with your heart as well as your ears. For example, a child may come in from play at dinner time, smell a particularly pungent and delicious dinner and rush to sit up, with his hands still black from mud-pies, saying 'I've washed my hands!'

If you lack empathy you may say something like 'That's a lie, and it's naughty to tell lies. You haven't washed them, look at them. Go and do it at once.'

If you have empathy you will understand how the whole episode happened. He came in obediently to your call and with every intention of carrying out the next bit of the dinner-time ritual, which was the washing of hands. But then his nose caught the aroma of whatever it was, which stimulated that part of his brain which said 'Food! Eat!' and the salivary glands began to secrete their juices. The strength of these primitive physical urges was stronger than the recently acquired habit of washing so he rushed straight to the table, and then when he was sitting up his eyes saw the tablecloth and forks and spoons and the mat for the hot dish to come, and suddenly he remembered that clean hands are part of all this preparation. He identified so closely with the feeling of 'clean hands' that fact and fantasy blurred and the words 'I've washed my hands!' were a way of saying 'Oh! help, bother, I should have washed, I know it now, but I want her to know that I've remembered before she tells me, and I haven't yet learned to master the complexities of the verb "to wash", so I can't say "I should have washed my hands", I can only say what I always say at this point, "I've washed my hands", and hope that she understands.'

Neither of you will stop to work it all out like this, but with empathy you won't need to because you will understand the way it was and will be able to offer him a way of putting things right without a fuss, such as 'Well, they still look a bit black to me, see if you can get them really clean while I dish up' or, if that isn't your way, then a cheerful 'Oh! no you didn't! Go on hop it, and don't come back until they're clean.' What matters from the child's point of view is that your words, tone of voice and whole demeanour convey to him that you understand how this lapse occurred, and that you aren't holding it against him.

Empathy adds a new dimension to living, and many previously insensitive people have acknowledged the debt of gratitude that they owe their children on this score. But it isn't something that just happens automatically. It has to be cultivated, and the spurs to learning are the genuine desire to understand your child, together with your own memories of what it feels like not to be understood.

My first holiday in France suddenly made me realise how a child must feel trying to make himself understood without an adequate command of language. When I went shopping I used to rehearse my various set pieces for each market stall, and choosing ones that were not busy I would edge near trying to catch someone's eye. The words never came out as I intended, but nods, smiles, pointing and a few isolated words (with no refinements such as verbs correctly conjugated) served the purpose well, and I felt wonderfully triumphant.

The stallholders were friendly and unfailingly helpful in seeing that I got what I wanted and that I understood the financial part of the transaction. They also gave me every encouragement to learn new words and phrases and I even began to talk about the weather, the sea and the sand. And then one of them began to correct my grammar, but it was too soon and I reverted to being anxious and afraid of trying in case I was wrong. I also learned that the Saturday market was neither the time nor the place to combine learning a language with doing the shopping. I was overlooked in the jostling crowd and felt ruffled, rejected and uncomfortably stupid, and I was mortified to discover how quickly I became childlike when put at a disadvantage. For a moment I even considered going back to enlist help with the equivalent of the cry 'Daddy do it'!

There are times when all parents feel as pressured as Saturday market stallholders, and a toddler learns to recognise those times and will either steer clear or whimper or shout for attention according to his own feelings at that time. But there are other times when a peaceful rapport will give him the confidence to experiment with words and phrases, and at these times it is important to share what he is trying to say without correcting his grammar. If he says 'I've beed in the garden', you can say 'You've been in the garden? I wondered where you were', and if he says 'We see Granny yesterday?' you can say 'Yes, we are going to see Granny, we are going to see her tomorrow when we have had one more sleep.' The correct use of words will come in time; what matters initially is the discovery of the joy and purposes of learning to talk.

You will learn to understand your child's speech long before anyone else, but some of you may have toddlers whose speech is unintelligible to anyone but you. Adults can lose their confidence just as quickly as children when a stream of meaningless sounds is directed at them, to which they are expected to reply. The tendency is for the stricken adult to look at the parent, who says in an aside 'He's trying to tell you that Fido ate one of his new slippers', but this means that the two adults are communicating with each other when it is the child who passionately wants to be able to communicate his own story. The spirit of the occasion can be preserved better if the one being regaled with the story listens with her face, nodding, smiling, raising an eyebrow and generally responding to the child's excitement as accurately as possible, whilst the mother or father backs him up rather than talks across him: 'He was a bad dog. Your lovely new slipper . . .

and he bit it, didn't he?' Then the relieved third party can respond by asking for further information about Fido (remembering that it will call forth another flood of excited sound), or offer information about another dog of her acquaintance, which makes the child feel valued and understood as a person. One or two simple questions relating to the story may encourage a single word response which adds to the lovely feeling that a real conversation is taking place, and nothing succeeds like success.

Some children have minds that race ahead of their tongues, and what may seem to be a speech defect is sometimes a child in such a hurry to communicate that although his intentions are clear the words are distorted. Others hardly speak at all, and strangely enough it is often equally helpful to children with both types of difficulty to arrange for a very quiet time when you can take them on your lap with a scrapbook in which there is only one picture on each page.

As each page is complete in itself there is no mounting excitement as a story builds up, and no demands on memory. On the contrary there is the need for a short pause to switch off from the previous picture before going on to the next one. The slowness and quietness of your voice will act as a brake, and in this companionable physical closeness words won't be terribly important so therefore the pressure on either type of child is minimal. Your running commentary can wander on along the lines of 'There's a lovely white cat, he's lucky to have that new carpet to lie on. And there's a kettle . . . we've got a kettle haven't we? What do we do with our kettle?' If the only sound is the contented sucking of a thumb then leave the question unanswered and slowly go on to the next picture.

Remember that the object of the exercise is to make it possible for the child to speak so naturally that he isn't even aware that he has spoken. There may come the desired moment when a contented voice says clearly 'Make tea' and you will have to smother your desire to say exultantly 'There! you *can* speak clearly' or 'There! you *have* got a tongue in your head' and control your voice to carry on evenly saying 'And look at this big dinner. I can see baked beans, and sausages . . .' With any luck the voice may come in again saying 'And peas, I don't like peas.'

Try to resist the temptation to tell relations and friends the good news in front of your child, or on the phone within earshot. Those who have succumbed to this very human temptation will tell you how self-consciousness clamped down on the child again and slowed progress to the general disappointment of everyone concerned.

Another hazard of this age and stage is that children convey a message perfectly clearly but not in the language of your choice. Jamie, aged two years and nine months, came out with 'Where my blimey boots are?' and, a month later, 'I not find my flaming clock!' Some parents are shocked, and some find this irresistably funny and laugh uproariously whilst repeating the sayings proudly to friends and neighbours in the child's hearing (only to be angry when he is old enough not to be considered 'cute'). Neither course is logical or helpful. A child will repeat what he hears, and if there are words that you don't want him to use you must first ask yourself if he hears them from you or someone else in the family. If they come from outside the family the wisest course is to ignore them and to repeat the sentence serenely without the offending words: 'Your boots are in the shed; we put all our muddy boots there don't we?' or 'Isn't your clock by your bed?' (if it is a real clock) or 'You will be late for work if you don't find it, where can it be?' (if it is a game of make believe). Swear words usually come to have a particular fascination only if children sense that by using them they can throw us into a state of shock and anxiety.

Another cause for distress is the conversation that accompanies behaviour that shocks us. Two small boys were in the lavatory together when a mother heard one say, 'Your wee sounds different to my wee.' Luckily for the children it just so happened that she thought it was marvellous that one of them had noticed the difference in sound when one weed into the water and the other on to the porcelain. This was a perfectly innocent occasion accompanied by a perceptive observation, and wisely nothing was said as the children flushed the lavatory and went to wash their hands. Another possible reaction would have been for the mother to say 'What are you doing? It's rude to be in there together, come on out.' The disapproval could have been so mystifying that the interest in the different sounds produced could have been obliterated, and the process of learning to learn could have been checked unnecessarily.

One quite frequent cause for concern is the youngest child of the family who doesn't learn to speak because everyone anticipates and provides for his every need. These children are usually quite capable of speech, it is almost as though they go through the inner motions of saying the words silently to themselves even when they don't need to utter them – and often as soon as the others are all at school the 'baby' begins to talk quite fluently. But if he has really been a contented passenger on the train of other people's thinking, speaking and acting, then it takes a little longer for him to speak up for himself once the others are away for the day.

Another characteristic of this age-group is the inability of some children to recognise themselves as 'I'. A $2\frac{1}{2}$-year-old saw a film of himself in which he cried. He watched it with no emotion and said as a statement of fact, 'Stuart's crying.' A year later he saw the film again and said as an equally calm statement of fact, 'I don't cry now.'

In much the same way children of this age-group can dissociate themselves from events. 'I didn't break the cup, I didn't' usually means 'I did break the cup, it was an accident, and now that it's done and I'm here, and the pieces are over there, it is quite easy to say "I didn't break the cup" – how could I have done with all that distance in time and space between me and it?' It bears repeating that what matters at this stage is for him to be encouraged to report all such mishaps without guilt or anxiety. If you didn't see the incident it isn't appropriate to express either belief or disbelief so the best policy is probably to say 'Come and show me, and we'll see if we can mend it.' When you arrive at the scene you can say 'I expect it was an accident' in the tone of voice that rightly implies that such things happen to all of us, and then you can either try to mend it together or put the pieces in the dustbin together.

If a child breaks something accidentally in front of you, and then shouts 'I didn't do it, I didn't do it!', it may indicate that in the past someone has been so cross about accidents that there is an instinctive need to disclaim responsibility through fear; or just occasionally it may be done in defiance to see just how far he can go before you impose the limits for which he longs (see the section on 'Aggression', p. 45).

If a child does something that he knows at once will be condemned as 'naughty' and then immediately says 'I've got a headache' or 'I've hurt my foot' or 'Look at my poor little finger!' then the chances are that he is used to people being cross with him, but he has learned that the one sure way to guarantee loving kindness and sympathy is to be ill. So he puts two and two together in the intricate processes of his mind and without being consciously aware of what is happening he will say in effect 'I've been naughty, I deserve your anger, but I don't like your anger, so here's a bit of me that is poorly. Please love the poor bit better first and then with any luck you'll forget about the naughty bit.' If the 'poor little me' approach is to be discouraged then it is important that in future displeasure isn't so great that he can't face it without evasion.

These are all ways in which your capacity to listen to

what lies behind the words will be challenged, but there will be other occasions when listening is an enchantment that calls for nothing more than a willingness to respond to the mood and the moment; times when a book, held upside down as likely as not, will be 'read' aloud in a nonsense language that yet has the rise and fall of your voice reading a story; times when lovely burblings break into a tone that is between talking and singing; times when a doll, toy or pet will be scolded, comforted or lulled to sleep with real or made-up words; times when your own sharp scolding voice will be clearly recognisable, and your I-told-you-so voice, and your I'll-make-it-better voice, and your I-love-you voice.

Later on there will probably be invented words, some of which may linger on in family usage for years to come, and imaginary members of the family who will become almost as real to you as they are to him, and vivid descriptions that take your breath away by their sheer poetry, as when a child looked at daffodils in an unexpected burst of sun and said 'They are too hot, and so they have opened their coats.'

The real world and his fantasies weave together in intricate patterns that we can't follow, and even to try to do so would sometimes be an infringement of his personal space. Sometimes you will see him listening intently to bird song, an aeroplane, a ticking clock, or even sitting still and gazing intently into space as though he is tuned in to something beyond our comprehension – which he may well be.

Learn to turn yourself off sometimes and take time to watch and listen quietly, for you see before you a new human being who has already learned more in his first two or three years than he will ever learn again in a comparable period of his life – and it is you who have made it possible.

Helping Each Other

Probably all of us have said to our toddlers at one time or another 'Are you coming to help me?' when what we really meant was 'If you come with me I shall know where you are and can keep an eye on you. Your "help" will slow me down, but better that than constantly having to stop what I'm doing to see what you're doing.' But at other times we really do enjoy the relationship between us as we work side by side in harmony, and although the 'help' may be slow it is genuinely helpful – such as handing us the pegs as we hang the washing on the line.

Ours is a materialistic and practical age and almost always our idea of help is associated with jobs done together instead of alone. But at a much deeper level we all need help from each other if we are to go on growing and developing towards our full stature as human beings. Some people are too proud to ask for help; some refrain from asking because they are afraid of being a nuisance; some ask for help constantly; and some can't bring themselves to ask for what they want because they were brought up to feel that this is selfish – 'You should give not take.' This attitude can often cause as much distress all round in the long run as the opposite one of satisfying our own needs all the time even if it is at the expense of other people.

All of us are affected to some degree by our own parents' attitudes, and before we hand them and our own on to children we need to pause and consider the matter quite carefully. It is difficult to see ourselves objectively but often we can look at our toddlers and see ourselves in them with a greater understanding of both of us.

If our toddlers are going to eat three meals a day then they need to be aware of, and share in, the work involved.

Rather than 'Would you like to help me clear the table?', it is more appropriate to say 'We must just clear the table before we go out, mustn't we? You take the salt cellar and I'll take the plates. Now let's get the other things.' We can't all 'decide' whether or not we want to do things because certain jobs for the family have to be done each day, they are not optional. There will be times when you decide to do a job alone for your own sake, or when you judge it isn't appropriate to involve your toddler for his sake, but when a task is shared do think about making it a matter of course sometimes rather than a matter of free choice. However much you may love the role of mother-provider or father-provider for the family, in these early years it is very bad for the children to be wholly on the receiving end of all this love and work.

Some families slowly evolve a system whereby everybody knows that they have to do a certain number of jobs for themselves every day and share others on a rota. Other families work on a system of helping each other to help each other: 'I think Dad would welcome an offer of help with . . .' Others rely on a developing sense of fair play. Some parents find it 'quicker to get on alone', or else make a conscious decision not to repeat their own childhood by 'making him grow up before his time', and then feel hurt when a request for help with the washing-up in later years results in a chorus of 'I did it last time. Do I *have* to? I've got to clean out the guinea pig. I don't see why I . . . it isn't fair that . . .'

When help is given it is only common courtesy to thank the helper, but the degree of thanks shouldn't be extravagantly effusive or indiscriminate at any age. Putting a dirty spoon on the draining board doesn't usually rate the same response as an anxious toddler calling out 'It's raining!' as he struggles to open the back door with the laundry basket in one hand on his way to rescue the washing from the line.

Another point to bear in mind when trying to promote

the idea that members of a family work for and with each other is that fathers at work are often genuinely forgotten: out of sight is out of mind at the toddler stage. It helps therefore to include them in your conversations together – 'Look at all the dirt on daddy's car duster! Let's wash it for him so that it's nice and clean again.'

As you think, plan, decide and work together you will become aware of your toddler's unique personality and attitude towards helping and being helped – which may reflect your own, or be brought about partly in response to your own, or be part of his own temperament. It isn't a question of 'fault' for we are all what we are, but neither is it a denial of the integrity of personality to learn to modify our actions and attitudes in the light of experience and insight. On the contrary, it is one of the hallmarks of our continuing growth and development for which we are often indebted to our children.

Some toddlers may draw back from a new job or experience for one of several reasons. Maybe they don't like the look of it. For example, some children love helping to wash the car, others don't like the look of hands disappearing into a bucket of dirty water. Or it may be that they so enjoy watching that they aren't yet ready to move on to the stage of becoming involved in 'doing'. I have great sympathy with these children, remembering how I watched and listened to the cows being milked, smelt the hay, cattlecake and milk, and was blissfully happy in the cowshed night and morning for years before I suddenly wanted to milk a cow myself. Remember your own particular childhood joys of watching, and if you see yourself in your child then let him watch to his heart's content (but if the watching seems to be apathetic instead of positively enjoyable then stimulation in small, happy doses is called for).

Sometimes these watching children long to join in but are too timid to take the plunge. Often all they need is gentle encouragement, but just sometimes it indicates that one or more members of the family may be so quick, bright and efficient that the toddler feels overshadowed and defeated before he even starts. If you feel there may be some truth in this for you then continue to work alone at your own speed, but make a point of slowing down for joint enterprises – and it helps if you sit with him instead of stand or lean over him, and speak slowly and quietly so that his own personality and capability has a chance to rise up until there is a feeling of equality between you. Also, be careful how you offer help to these diffident children for the 'Here, give it to me, I'll do it' type of help lowers their self-esteem still further: it takes longer but is more effective to consider whatever it is together, to share the job, and to boost their confidence by legitimate recognition and praise for their part in the undertaking.

Occasionally a child is referred to affectionately or with exasperation as 'lazy', but laziness isn't a natural characteristic of children so alternative reasons for non-involvement should be considered. The child may be slow and stolid by nature, or a thinker rather than a doer, or he may not be getting enough fresh air and exercise to oxygenate his blood and stimulate his muscles, or his diet may be unbalanced in such a way that he is overweight but lethargic. His confidence may have been so undermined that he would rather not try at all than try and be found wanting, or he may be lonely for friends of his own age. (How often have you felt too tired to do anything only to be immediately recharged with energy by an unexpected invitation or visitor?)

Another very possible reason may be that he has been waited on hand and foot since birth to the point where he has been rendered passive. He may truly feel that the way to get things done is to 'ask nicely' or to 'wait a minute' until his willing and devoted slave gets round to doing the job for him. This isn't as far-fetched as it may sound because for some parents their relationship with their child is the first one that has given them prolonged emotional satisfaction, and it is their joy to give and give and give with no thought of reward beyond the welcome smiles and cuddles that greet each appearance and service. Often it is the advent of the second baby that is the rude awakening for both parent and toddler, for there just isn't the time or energy to do as much for him as before. In fact at this stage the mother genuinely needs his help sometimes. From the toddler's point of view he is fed up with this unrewarding, noisy, time- and attention-consuming object that has taken up residence and usurped his place at the centre of the universe. Things can go from bad to worse. The toddler becomes demanding and aggressive, and the mother is overtired, overwrought and deeply hurt that the longed-for 'perfect relationship' has let her down yet again – and replaces her hopes in the new baby.

So bear in mind the possibility that the cry 'He's lazy' may be followed later by 'He's spoilt' or 'He's jealous', to be followed in turn by 'I can't do anything with him', and that we just may have brought it upon ourselves by our excess of love! In love there has to be giving and receiving on both sides, and set limits.

Toddlers' reactions to being helped are just as varied as their attitudes to helping us. When all is going well they take a natural delight in learning to master new skills and then derive additional satisfaction from repeating them again and again. Sometimes their patience and confidence falters in an effort to master yet another skill, and they will leave it and go back to an earlier one as though to reassure themselves. If they could put it all into words we might hear them chuntering, 'I can't do that stupid shoe. It won't open its mouth wide enough for me to get my foot in. And the silly strings get in the way. I'm getting all cross. I know! I'll put on my bedroom slippers.' The same thing happens in their play. They master a puzzle, try a new one, but often keep breaking off to do and re-do the old one. Tiredness or overexcitement can also cause them to regress, and on such occasions the putting away of toys that they can manage perfectly well on their own each night may be beyond them, so either we offer help or risk aggravating the situation until it leads to temper or tears of frustration. Our example of kindness and understanding is more valuable than insistence on the rules at such times.

Illness and convalescence also cause regression and children often revert to playing with toys they outgrew some time ago. A visit to stay with relatives, or in a strange place, can have the same effect. One four-year-old reacted by asking for his bedroom light to be left on. His mother said mildly 'I don't think you really want it on now that you're a big boy, do you?' and his reply was 'I'm not a big boy tonight, I'm small and grumpy.'

Some children reach a stage of not wanting to be helped over anything, and if they proudly reject help we should let them struggle on alone until they succeed or give up, and if they eventually have to give up we can lessen the blow to their self-esteem by warmly praising them for trying so hard for so long.

If they are afraid to ask for help for fear of being a nuisance we should ask ourselves why this is so, for this isn't the way it should be. A more natural response was that of a three-year-old who had been very ill for three days and nights with her mother in constant attendance. The child woke from a feverish sleep in the early hours of the morning and asked for a drink; her mother lifted her up and held the cup to her lips; the child had a few sips and then met her mother's eyes and said 'I'm sorry.' Her mother said 'It's all right darling, I love you', and the child said simply 'I know.'

If they ask for help constantly, then we also need to ask ourselves questions: is this another result of our having rendered them passive? Or have they no confidence in their own ability? Or is it a habit? Or do they need more of our time and attention, and is this an indirect way of trying to bring us to their side more or less spontaneously?

Another facet of helping each other concerns our attitude and theirs to accidents. The first time a child breaks a cup the noise, the sheer surprise of it all, and the shock of seeing what the cup has turned into are often enough to reduce a child to tears. This is helpful to everyone, for even if the cup was a best one the sight of the sobbing child prompts parents to say 'It's all right, never mind, it was an accident', and the dustpan and brush are fetched and the pieces are carefully swept up as the stricken child looks on. Unfortunately it doesn't always work like this. The accident may be the last straw at the end of a bad day; it may have been a sentimentally precious cup; the child may be defiant instead of tearful, and the reaction may be 'You naughty boy, just look what you've done!' But if this pattern becomes a habit everyone could be heading for the spiral whereby the child hides the evidence of the next breakage because he can't face that degree of blame and anger. The pieces are found with the accusing question 'Who did this?' Then comes the ultimatum: 'If you own up I won't be cross, but if you tell a lie you'll get a smack.'

The crisis is so acute that one of several things usually happens. The child bursts into tears and the parental heart softens at that coupled with the relief that the child has 'owned up'; or the child wants to own up but the pressure is so great that he can't get a word out (which may be interpreted as stubbornness or defiance); or confrontation has happened so many times before that already the child is learning to brazen it out because he can't afford to admit to himself that he really is as worthless as everyone seems to think.

We are only human and of course we shall be cross and upset sometimes, but if it is possible it really does pay to concentrate on the breakage rather than the breaker – and to try to repair the damage. Children need to learn that we all have accidents, that our first consideration is whether or not anyone has been hurt, that the second is whether or not it can be put right, and that the third is either to try to effect a repair or to dispose of the pieces in the dustbin. In this way children grow up not needing to hide their mistakes (except sometimes!) and with the habit of trying to rectify them if possible. The habit begins to become an attitude of mind so that when things go wrong distress is followed more easily by acceptance and ability to cope rather than by lashing out physically or verbally, trying to put the blame somewhere, or taking it out on someone else.

Once toddlers begin to associate the idea of 'helping', with the multiple pleasures of enjoying jobs for their own sake, and the feeling of being needed, and the harmony of the working relationship, and the satisfaction of being appreciated and depended upon, then inevitably there are problems as well as pleasures. What do you do when you find the wash-basin has been cleaned as a surprise, only with talcum instead of cleaning powder? Or when potatoes in their jackets have been scrubbed very clean, with soap? We can't have it both ways. If they help they will also hinder through ignorance or accident, but if they are eager to help and want to feel useful their offerings and efforts need to be accepted in the spirit in which they are intended, and if their good idea is a disaster we should still at least try to acknowledge and accept that their *intention* was to be helpful.

Sharing the Homemaking

Every family needs somewhere to call home, for home is the physical and emotional shelter for the family, and in every home there are innumerable jobs that have to be done that all add up to homemaking, which is infinitely more than housekeeping. The doing and coordinating of all these jobs is the essential background to the central job of raising and nurturing a family, and every member of the family (and society) should recognise that this mammoth task calls for creative intelligence, sensitivity, an aptitude for work and responsibility, endurance and a capacity for caring about other people. These qualities are lived and transmitted, caught rather than taught from generation to generation, and if homemaking is once again to be esteemed as the essential art it is then right from their earliest days children need to associate the various jobs to be done with happy memories of their parents and homes.

During my years working, playing and staying with playgroup families all over the country, one of the greatest joys has been listening to parents talk about children, and helping them to recall their own earliest childhood. Some of their happiest memories are so common that it is worth recording them, partly as a jog to individual memories (so often people said 'I'd forgotten all about that until you reminded me'), and partly to offer the ideas for consideration to those who have no such memories.

North and south, town and country, one of these memories is of what followed when mothers (or others) said 'Let's go and make the beds.'

Some families now have duvets, and some don't make the beds until they crawl thankfully into them at night, but for those who still have sheets and blankets and make the beds as part of their daily routine the remembered play ritual was based on two themes – lost and found, and darker and lighter.

In the former the child would hide under the pile of stripped bedclothes at the end of the bed, keeping still and quiet as the voice above said 'I wonder where Lucy can be? Perhaps she's under this sheet . . . No . . .', and so it continued as the bed was deftly made to the last cover. At this point there was an alternative: either 'Well, she must be under this one. Hooray!', in which case there was a joyful hugging session, or 'I think she must be lost . . . boo hoo', in which case there was a comforting session.

The other game started with the child helping to smooth and tuck in the bottom blanket and sheet and plumping up the pillows. Then she got into the bed and lay very still (this was important for a riotous game defeated the serious need to complete a job properly). First the sheet was pulled right up and over her face (be careful about this lest the child be frightened), then the first blanket, then the second as the voice said 'Now it's getting darker . . . and darker . . . and darker . . .'; then it was time to turn the tops down as the voice said 'And now it's getting lighter . . . and lighter . . . and lighter . . . and there you are!' The getting-out bit had to be managed carefully in case the nicely made bed was spoiled, and an extra smoothing of the pillows and covers indicated that bedmaking was a proper job to be done well.

During those games the children certainly didn't help to make the beds, but it was a help to the bedmaker to have a happy child who wasn't getting into mischief elsewhere. The children were also beginning to build up memory banks of information about bedmaking that would be tried out later on dolls' beds and prams (which is why boys as well as girls will want to try it out – it is partly a memory game). All these play stages are needed as a forerunner of learning to make their own beds eventually.

Another job that is remembered with pleasure is sorting

the washing. Sometimes it was 'whites in one heap, coloured in the other'; sometimes it was 'socks here, shirts there, bed linen here'; later on it was 'cottons here, woollens there'. Everyone remembered wondering how ever anyone could tell the difference between materials other than the simple distinction between 'knitted and not knitted', and now man-made fibres have added to the difficulty.

Some parents won't like the idea of children handling dirty clothes. Some won't be able to bear seeing clothes strewn all over the floor. Some will have toddlers who aren't interested anyway. Some will have toddlers who are side-tracked into a game of their own with the contents of the clothes basket, which they may or may not be allowed to continue. But some parents may be glad to be reminded of a 'game' that they enjoyed and will probably remember that the final satisfaction was to crawl into the empty clothes basket (safely on its side on the floor) in time to be discovered with the cry 'Well, what's this that needs washing!'

Spring-cleaning the pantry or larder is another happy memory with many common elements, even though some recall a cupboard under the stairs whilst others visualise a farmhouse walk-in room with stone floors and slate slab shelves laden with food and dotted with mousetraps. Quite often now a refrigerator and a shelf in a cupboard take the place of either. The common memories are of packets, tins and jars being transferred to the kitchen table to be inspected, sniffed, thrown away or put into clean jars and rearranged neatly on the newly washed shelves.

Whether you have a walk-in pantry or a small cupboard your toddler can share your periodic reorganisation, and even if you hadn't thought of doing the job a wet day may well decide you to undertake it as a profitable way for both of you to be usefully employed.

Toddlers love fetching and carrying, and most can be

a real help in taking things from you and putting them where you suggest. They won't be able to place glass jars on top of the table, but can put packets and tins into washing-up bowls, on to trays, or into boxes on the kitchen floor as you direct. They can tip the contents of jars into separate bowls, and when the jars have been washed and dried they can transfer the contents back into the clean jars. This is a tricky operation and it pays to deal with one bowl at a time, putting sugar, lentils, sultanas or what-ever on to a tray, together with the clean jar and suitable implements for each particular transfer.

Lentils can be ladled into an egg cup with a teaspoon, and then tipped into the jar – and if orange lentils become boring then interest may perk up with yellow split peas. Caster sugar can be spooned into a small jug, and then poured into the clean container. Macaroni and sultanas can be dropped by hand through a wide funnel. Each operation is an absorbing form of play yet with an underlying work purpose.

The play progress is likely to be so slow that you will have time to wash the shelves and replace the larger items before the play-work is completed, but let him carry his own jars into their place of honour even if you feel your particular toddler needs to carry them in a basket, one at a time, for his safety and theirs.

At this age and stage, even if he started the pantry operation with the idea of 'helping', this will soon be lost in 'play', but when he sees the jars back on your clean shelves then you can remind him of how hard you have both 'worked' to make everything look so nice.

Shoe cleaning evokes mixed memories because it is one of the jobs that children sometimes undertake alone to 'surprise' their parents, with disastrous results. Toddlers know (eventually) that you put newspaper down on the floor when you want to clean your shoes, but how is he to know the difference between yesterday's and today's paper? Cleaning shoes looks fun, and he wants to help you, but having watched your deft movements how can he know that black polish is black? You put it on straight out of the tin, on a black brush, on to black shoes, and after a bit of brushing they shine. He tries it, and suddenly his hands are black, and so is everything he touches. Why? He is as surprised as you are horrified. Neutral shoe cream is safer to begin with. Alternatively, put the polish on yourself, and let your toddler brush it off.

So many mistakes come about through innocent ignorance on his part – and on ours, because we simply didn't see how things looked to him as he watched us.

Most people associate cooking with pastry and the left-over pieces to play with. But cake making has its own memories, pride of place going to 'licking out the bowl'. Some remember literally putting their heads in the bowl to lick out the last of the beautiful sweet creamy mixture, and then emerging with hair so sticky that it had to be washed straight away; others remember scraping every last vestige clean with a teaspoon.

Even if you usually buy cakes, or have an electric mixer, it is worth going back to making cakes by hand occasionally. Baking in the old-fashioned way is very satisfying for children because it is slow, requires physical effort, and registers through their senses of touch, sight, taste, smell and hearing. It is worth remembering this on one of those days when you can't go out, or when a bored toddler is infinitely more tiring than making a cake by hand together.

Many parents' memories of cake making are particularly happy – as one put it 'Not exciting-happy but peaceful-happy' – and many associate this quality of peacefulness with the fact that their mothers had a special baking day, wore special clothes and a special apron, and stayed quietly in one place until the job was done.

Some remember the bowl with the margarine or butter and sugar being set by the fire to warm before the creaming together began. Others recall it being put in the airing cupboard or boilerhouse, or being stood in a bowl of hot water, or put in a very slow oven. All can remember the times when it was left too long and the fat turned into a golden liquid, and all can then recall other times when liquid butter solidified again but looked, felt and even tasted different. The weighing and sifting of flour, the pinch of salt, the addition of dried fruit, cocoa or chocolate powder, coconut, lemon or orange juice and grated peel, and the breaking and beating of eggs – all these memories come back with a mixture of nostalgia for the occasion and vivid sensory memories of the ingredients and processes involved. The combination of the two laid the foundations for learning not just about cake making but about homemaking, and the value of happy memories of childhood is that they can be passed on to the next generation.

Other strong cooking memories are centred on casseroles and vegetables. Many a child was allowed to play with the cubes of vegetables under the impression that he was packing the casserole. He might group the vegetables by colour – white turnips, yellow parsnips, orange swedes, dark orange carrots – then the coloured piles could be put in one at a time, or one from each pile could be put in by turns. The child felt he was 'helping' but was also enjoying leisurely and valuable play along the way, and learning about the vegetables into the bargain. Carrots are almost always the first to be recognised by name, perhaps because of their colour and the distinctive inner circle of a different shade, and because of the sweet taste when eaten raw.

Most, too, remember rolling the pieces of meat in seasoned flour, and some even remember sitting on the scrubbed wooden kitchen table in order to arrange everything in the big earthenware pot more easily.

Undeniably it will be quicker for you to say 'Run along and play while I just get the dinner ready', but you will be depriving your toddler of so much happy satisfaction

212

and learning if he doesn't work and play alongside you quite often.

Scrubbing is another happy memory for many parents and even though there are few wooden tables and floors to scrub these days there are still other scrubbing opportunities. Potatoes can be scrubbed and pricked ready for the oven; balconies of flats, doorsteps and sinks can be scrubbed with large bristle nailbrushes or a shoe-cleaning brush kept specially for the purpose (nylon tufts don't give the same satisfaction that comes from the 'give' of pliable bristles).

The fluctuating rhythm of work and play was beautifully understood by a mother who set her two- and four-year-old daughters to scrub the doormat 'well' by the back door. She provided a small plastic bowl containing about three inches of warm water, an adult scrubbing brush each and a cake of soap each. They scrubbed away side by side for ages, making patterns in the soap suds and breathing heavily with sheer effort. Then the bigger one said 'Aren't we hard [working] ladies?' The little one said 'Yes!' Then the bigger one expressed her state of bliss by saying 'I'll do what Mummy says for ever and ever', and the little one echoed 'So will I.'

After working up to that state of bliss there was nowhere to go but down, and shortly afterwards the exchanges were typical of children growing tired both physically and emotionally: 'Your brush hit me . . . you're on my bit . . . that's my soap . . . no it's mine . . . it's mine . . . it's *mine*.' Then the little one threw down her brush and said 'I shan't play any more' (they had been 'working' when they were at the peak of enjoyment), then she threw down her soap, and it skidded right out of the well. There was the silence of sheer surprise, then peals of laughter, and the play took on a new lease of life for several more minutes before they got up saying 'We've finished now.'

The children took their brushes and soap back to the

kitchen; the bigger one carried the bowl; their mother removed the surplus soap suds and opened the door to let the concrete dry; then she shook and replaced the mat because the children had lost interest. But when their father came home she said 'Are you going to show Daddy what you did today?' and they rushed to show him and glowed with pride in his praise.

It takes time, imagination and nervous energy to help children, and to help them to help us, but it is the sharing of our time, and our tasks, and ourselves, with them that they want and need above everything else. Think back to your own earliest childhood, and if you still have your parents ask them to remind you of your toddler days. Share your memories with brothers and sisters, friends and relations, and you will probably find that more and more flashes of early experience come back to you, and as they do so you may be able to remember how you actually felt at the time. These memories of what you did, and what you felt like, and how you felt about your parents' reactions, can be a very valuable bridge between the three generations: you will have a greater sympathy with your toddler, and also with your parents.

Recall all the happy memories you can, and pass them on to your children, and then go on to invent new ones based on gadgets, man-made materials and new patterns of mothering and fathering that your parents and grandparents may not have known. And ask yourself what happy memories of 'helping' your toddler is likely to pass on to his own children eventually, for homemaking can never be a static art.

You Don't Have to be Alone

A mother writes:

'The child you expect is a statement of love and affection. More pure than any other because it is yours and you know it.

'The child you love is new and flimsy – more precious than any other. A proud new toy, new acquisition. Parenthood is going to be hard – every one says so, but you won't let it change your life too much. Nothing but the best for them of course, new pram, pretty cot.

'After four weeks you count his age in months not days or weeks and he keeps you awake at night and does change your life a lot. No outings in the evening, a lot more shopping and washing and worst of all – isolation. It doesn't matter about not going out in the evenings as a child is adequate compensation in itself but the worst is to be alone with no one to talk to – except about babies. No grandmothers at home – they are at work – no sisters or brothers or childless wives. All are at work. If this was not bad enough in itself the not so noticed implication is that they are earning money while using their hands and/ or minds. Thus those who need to have clothes for their children, and well fitting shoes and all that good healthy food they promised themselves their children would have, cannot afford it. Life becomes frugal, nothing left for clothes or holidays, the latter being very badly needed in view of sleepless nights and the monotony of a boring day.

'There are compensations as they grow older, you can have fun doing painting with them or telling about tadpoles and flowers, birds and trees. Even better, they begin to talk and want to learn. *But* they empty things out of cupboards, have wandering hands, waste paper, pinch treasures, break treasures, flood the bathroom, dig up plants, get sand in the carpet, footprints on the ceiling!

'Is that really me I can hear shrieking at the top of my voice? Using words I always swore I never would? Thwarting their creative talents or instincts by saying they can't have the paint because it gets everywhere or the Lego because they never pick it up and I am always treading on it? Is it me saying I won't read them a story because I haven't got time, and parking them in front of frightful American cartoons on the television instead? I am afraid it is. It must be because I never get a moment to myself, for thought, or to read the paper.

'Everything done has to be cursory because the children get bored. Visits to museums are twenty-minute jobs, and art galleries even less, one quick glance if you're lucky. This is the worst frustration – the inability to pursue any interest or thought to a satisfactory conclusion. A constant bombardment of mind and body by questions and requests, of the ears by whining and yelling. But any mother knows this.

'I am sure that my children are much more badly behaved than any others, especially in public. Always running off in the shops and disarranging supermarket shelves, or howling for sweets. (That is one principle I have managed to stick to – not giving in at the sweet shop or the sweet shelves by the checkout in the supermarket!)

'It seems to be only my children that say they won't walk any farther, and crumple their legs up when both hands are laden with heavy carrier bags cutting into the fingers. It looks so awful to assist them to their feet with your foot, but it's the only free limb available! The ultimate horror is in the bank – one is scribbling on the blotter (to black looks from the manager) and the other shoots out of the door to the road while the cashier is just counting the money and there is a large impatient queue behind you. Do you leave the child or the money?

'If only shopkeepers would take it upon themselves to tell children off. They seem afraid to do it these days (they weren't when I was little) and yet children would listen to them far more readily than to their own mothers.

'All this I can bear. What is worst is to lose my temper, I feel this is failure. Worse still, to be reduced to smacking them as much as I do. It seems to have become habit instead of the very last resort. Every now and again I become aware of it and try new tactics, but I am ashamed to admit that bribery and reasoning just don't have any effect. Perhaps I just don't have the patience to carry things through. I feel guilty. What must everyone think of all the shouting and banging? I hate to hear it from others. Perhaps some parents just don't have quite the right temperament for parenthood (my husband is even worse).

'But it is nice to have an excuse for visiting the zoo and going to toy shops. It is so nice when they sit quietly and listen and remember. It is rewarding when they make sensible statements. And just simply being a family is most reassuring, especially when they love and kiss you despite all you have said, done, or stopped them from doing.

'Is there any parent brave enough to take their children for lunch in a restaurant?

'Don't imagine I dislike being a parent, I just feel a failure at it, and on top of that, frustrated and mentally unfulfilled. How awful to admit that one of the best times is when they are peacefully and angelically asleep, then you feel that you can't have done quite *everything* wrong!'

This mother will speak for and to many of you, and you are all a hopeful sign for the future. There was a period when young marrieds really did believe the myth of 'And they lived happily ever after', and looked forward to 'the radiant fulfilment of motherhood'. Disillusionment was so great that individual and collective disenchantment set in, and the pendulum was in danger of swinging too far the other way as some individuals in women's lib.

rendered a disservice to their vital cause by trying to propagate the opposite myth of motherhood as a drudgery and an infringement of personal liberty. Now there is a breath of honesty in the air, and between these two extremes people are beginning to face not just facts but basic truths about marriage, parenthood and life itself – and one of the toughest of these truths is that although we can know suffering without love (and very embittering it can be), there is no way we can experience love without suffering.

No human life can grow and develop towards its full potential without experiencing the range of feeling between happiness and sadness, hope and despair, success and failure, exhilaration and exhaustion, frustration and fulfilment, and love and suffering. Most of us hope to die with the feeling that we have realised at least a good measure of our potential, that our lives justified our existence, and that when the time comes we shan't die with the feeling that we have never really lived. We do matter in the scheme of things, and it isn't selfish to want to experience fulfilment, but there is a strange paradox in that if we deliberately set out to find this fulfilment as an end in itself it often eludes us. It finds us, rather than we find it, as we are able to let go of ourselves for the sake of those we love.

Yet there is another paradox, for if we become martyrs then the self is so denied that emptiness or warping can result, so a balance has to be found whereby we can make the sacrifices that are inevitably part of parenthood without becoming martyrs. And even then we can't keep it up all the time and need others who will also be prepared to fill us up with the same degree of self-giving.

Perhaps at no other time in our lives is it so important for us to accept the idea of being a *lively* sacrifice as it is during the early years of motherhood and fatherhood, yet this is the very time when husbands and wives may find it most difficult to meet the ceaseless demands made upon them by babies and toddlers. The change from carefree young marrieds to parents can seem so final; it may distress both of them to discover that mothers at this stage often find it difficult to feel and behave like mistresses, and it seems as though the day-long vigilance and the broken nights will go on for ever leaving no energy or spontaneity for love-making. There is often one pay-packet instead of two, and the lack of financial independence can lead to a lack of self-respect in some wives (this needs to be talked about more freely for the husband's sincere 'But it isn't my money, it's our money' doesn't quite take into account the wife's reluctance to ask for something that was once hers because she had earned it in the conventional way). There is a great sense of loneliness for many mothers who have been used to working with others, and a frustration in never being able to chat and laugh on equal terms with a toddler as they once did with their colleagues and workmates. Fathers, too, can experience a loneliness for male companionship at a time when home seems to be an essentially female province, and wise wives know that husbands need a great deal of physical contact with, and responsibility for, their babies and toddlers if they are to feel like fathers.

All in all, it isn't surprising that so many young mothers find themselves in the doctor's surgery asking very sensibly for help, but meanwhile society is at last coming to recognise the fact that even the happiest, most capable and well adjusted, most confident and philosophical of parents (and parent substitutes) need relief from the strain of being on duty for twenty-four hours a day, seven days a week, fifty-two weeks of the year. Even those who didn't think they were missing anything have often found that they have felt brighter and more alive after encountering other parents and toddlers.

You may feel that there is absolutely nothing available in your area, and sadly this may be true, but more often than not at least some facilities are there though you may not know what they are or how to make contact. A fairly comprehensive list may be helpful. Even though you may never need most of the organisations yourself there may be friends and neighbours who would be glad to know of their existence.

In the case of national organisations the addresses are included so that the central staff can put you in touch with local branches or individuals, but you may be able to find what you are looking for on the board in the library, at the town hall, at the citizen's advice bureau, in the telephone book, or the local paper, or from the vicar or priest.

Since you may be hoping for another child it is worth starting at the beginning, but there is no significance in the order after that except that it ends with the happy and informal suggestions that are spreading through the country like wildfire.

Ante-natal Clinics

It is important to visit your local clinic regularly, even if you have already had a baby and feel confident and well. There is no substitute for trained and experienced medical supervision when it comes to making an early diagnosis of anything in you or your baby that needs attention.

The National Childbirth Trust (NCT)
9 Queensborough Terrace, London W2 3TB.

Increasingly husbands and wives together are attending their ante-natal, relaxation and information classes in order that both shall understand what is happening during pregnancy, and that the husband shall be prepared (if he wishes) to be with his wife during labour.

The friendships made during these classes are often carried on afterwards, and members of the NCT are slowly forming a support network over the country so that any mother suffering from 'baby blues' or loss of confidence can pick up the phone at any hour during the day or night and be sure of an understanding listening ear Whenever it is possible a reassuring visit can be made and often the knowledge that someone else has been through it all before is enough to reassure the new mother (But if it isn't then a visit to the doctor may be helpful.)

Attendance at NCT classes should be in addition to not instead of, regular visits to your ante-natal clinic.

Post-natal Clinics

Once the baby has arrived, and especially if you have a toddler in tow, it isn't easy to make the effort to get into the clinic for the recommended check-up. But the more exhausted and back-aching you feel the more important it is to go – people can't help you if they don't know that things are beginning to get you down. Some people want pills for everything, others won't touch them, but I can still remember the relief of being told that I was anaemic (it wasn't just me being neurotic), and the difference that the course of pills made to my energy (don't rush off and buy iron pills over the counter, part of the cure is saying out loud just how you feel, and the diagnosis may not be the same for you as it was for me on that occasion).

Welfare Clinics

With a second baby you will be confident and familiar with the clinic routine, *and more alert to the needs of new mothers*. Do chat with them, but above all listen. This is not to suggest that you give them the advice that should properly come from a doctor or health visitor, but that you should share with them what it *feels* like to be alone all day with a new human being for whom you are responsible. You will find that memories come flooding back, and you will want to pass on the warmth and friendliness that you probably needed in those early months. I visited a clinic in a communicare centre recently and there were two rows of mothers sitting on opposite sides of a corridor, each cuddling her baby and no one saying a word. They were shy, not unfriendly, and it seemed tragic that they had all come along alone from the big housing estate, and that as they left the doctor's room they all walked out and went home alone.

A year later a mother and toddler club was established in this centre into which the pregnant mothers were welcomed on their ante-natal visiting days. The idea was to help them to make friends with each other, to become familiar with the sight, sound and behaviour of babies and toddlers if they had had no previous experience, and to make friends with mothers a stage ahead of themselves so that they had a point of reference if they needed it later on.

In many clinics now there are toys available for the toddlers to play with, and many a mother has picked up ideas for home play that are cheap and easy, or already available in the home, such as saucepan lids and wooden spoons.

The National Children's Bureau (NCB)
7 Wakely Street, Islington, London EC14 7QE.

Children develop at very different rates, but if you are at all worried about your child's physical or mental development do go and see your family doctor, health visitor, or family health centre doctor. There may be nothing wrong and your mind will be set at rest, or you may have drawn attention to something which needs appropriate help and action. Physical and mental handicap can often be lessened if action is taken early.

If you have a handicapped child, and even if you are already in touch with your family doctor, health visitor, or perhaps a social worker, do write to the NCB and ask for their excellent free booklet *Help Starts Here*, which is full of information that will help you to be sure you are contacting all the services which may be able to help you. These may be statutory (hospitals, clinics, social services, education) or voluntary services for the handicapped. There are four pages listing the names and addresses of just some of the organisations which may be able to help you, and if you would like fuller information about any of them then just write and ask, and additional details will be provided whenever possible. A book-list can also be obtained from the NCB.

An opportunity playgroup may help both you and your child. This is a playgroup for handicapped children which includes normal children and their parents to the great benefit of everyone – or a mother and toddler club or playgroup which often include one or two handicapped children. Your social services or local branch of the Pre-school Playgroups Association may be able to put you in touch with one that suits you.

The Toy Libraries Association
Seabrook House, Wyllyotts Manor, Darkes Lane, Potters Bar, Herts EN6 2HL.

If your child is handicapped write also to this association which will put you in touch with your nearest toy library where you can not only borrow ordinary and specially designed toys, but will be able to meet other parents with a similar experience to your own. Comparing can be both comforting and stimulating.

The National Council for One-parent Families
225 Kentish Town Road, London NW5.

This Council exists to speak up for and protect the interests of one-parent families at government level, and to keep such needs before the public. You may want to contact them at this level, or you may need a local support system, and this you are likely to find in Gingerbread.

The Gingerbread Association
35 Wellington Street, London WC2.

Parenthood is difficult enough when there are two to share the joys and burdens, but a single parent – either mother or father – has an overwhelming burden to carry. Local Gingerbread members are wonderfully supportive to each other, not least because they can share what it feels like to be deserted, or driven out, or to have faced the death of a partner, or to have wanted the baby but not marriage to the father. There are so many different reasons for being a one-parent family, and almost all of them inflict deep scars on the personality that need understanding and friendship as well as time to heal.

Gingerbread also has information about legal matters, such as supplementary benefits, maintenance orders, pensions, etc., and a local member will not only explain these to you but accompany you to the various officials concerned if you wish.

The National Association for the Welfare of Children in Hospital (NAWCH)
Exton House, 7 Exton Street, London SE1 8UE.

Increasingly now hospitals are trying to make it possible for at least one parent to stay in hospital with their child. Many paediatricians feel that this is particularly import-ant when a baby is kept in a special unit at birth, and at least one makes it a rule that the mother, and the father too if possible, shall see and touch the baby every day until it is time to go home together. He says that it is almost always possible for contact to be made with a hand or foot, and he shares the conviction of many that if physical contact isn't made in these early days then something is lost that it is difficult to restore. (Don't panic, many fathers came back from the war to be greeted by their children of three or four whom they had never seen before and, although it took time, many of them came to enjoy a particularly satisfying relationship with their children.) Under-fives have a particular need not to feel 'deserted' and many parents feel convinced that no child should be left alone to face the ordeal of a strange place, strange people and strange procedures.

If you feel like this, and your hospital doesn't welcome parents readily, then NAWCH may be able to help you.

Parents Anonymous (PA)

North Islington Welfare Centre, 6–9 Manor Gardens, Holloway Road, London N7 6LA.

This association exists to help parents who feel frightened, guilty, depressed or worried about difficulties with their children, from babies to adolescents. Every single one of us is capable of child abuse or neglect under certain circumstances: it may be a single act of violence, or repeated violence, or emotional neglect, or rejection of one child when all the others are loved, or difficulties of a different nature altogether. Whatever it is, you are not alone. If you live in an area where PA has a branch, you can pick up a telephone and talk to someone anonymously: it helps to talk.

In some areas there is already a 24-hour telephone service, and the phone will be answered by a parent who, although not necessarily trained in the professional sense, will have been through some of your experiences and will have been specially prepared for this particular anonymous telephone service.

Whatever the caller says will be accepted with under-

standing and without judgement, and often the relief of
being able to talk freely is all that is needed. If you want
to ask for professional help, names, addresses and telephone numbers will be available. If you would like the
helper to contact any of the agencies on your behalf, then
that will be done too – but this will never be done without
your permission.

If there isn't a branch of PA in your area you may have
a similar service called Helpline, Friends Anonymous or
some other equally descriptive name.

If you are feeling desperate now their Hotline phone
number is 01-669 8900.

'Slimming Magazine', Slimming Club, Weight Watchers, or the Silhouette Slimming Club

This may seem an odd intrusion in the list, but experience
indicates that it is very relevant for some mothers who put
on a lot of weight during pregnancy and can't seem to
stop the scales creeping up still further.

Some mothers can produce their babies and walk out
of the hospital wearing their honeymoon slim-line slacks;
others feel as though they are still pregnant and have to
continue to wear their maternity clothes. One thing leads
to another – the demands of a new baby leave them too
tired to go for a daily walk and depression about the
weight increase leads to nibbling for comfort. Added to
this an upbringing of not wasting food impels them to eat
left-overs after meals. The pounds and even stones pile
on and cause real misery; crash diets never work for long,
and are invariably followed by eating binges, to be
followed yet again by remorse and self-dislike, which in
turn lead to more comfort snacks.

If this is your pattern, buy *Slimming Magazine* each
month and ask for a subscription to one of your local
slimming clubs as a birthday present. Once the plunge is

made you will find many other people just like you, and knowing that you are not alone with your problem will reassure you immensely as you all get down to the job of slimming together. I have known so many people who say that it has revolutionised their lives to feel alert and confident again, and all of them wish they hadn't left it so long (though I have a theory that 'wishing' isn't enough and that it takes a real jolt to bring about this sort of positive decision and the determination to carry it through). But *don't* start slimming too soon after the birth of your baby, particularly if you are breast-feeding, and do check with your doctor first.

One o'clock Clubs

Playleadership Manager, 233 High Holborn, London WC1.

These clubs provide the opportunity for under-fives to play creatively and at the same time give the adults with them either the chance to sit and relax or to be involved in the activities of the children. Most of these clubs are in the Greater London Council parks but there are also a number on housing estates, and the idea is just beginning to spread to other towns.

One o'clock club buildings vary in size and type but all have heating, lighting and hot and cold water supplies, and they are always set in an enclosed area surrounded by a low fence so that there is ample space to play but with no risk of the children straying too far.

Each club has a senior playleader, usually assisted by two assistants and a trainee. There is no payment for the use of the club and no attendance register. Children accompanied by adults can come and go as they like in informal friendliness (but the adults must stay with and be responsible for their children all the time). The clubs are open from 1 p.m. to 4.30 p.m., Mondays to Fridays.

Play facilities include sand and water, paints, clay and

dough, books, table and floor toys and quiet corners for imaginative play. Out of doors are climbing-frames, trucks, a sandpit and an area for more active, energetic enjoyment, and a first chance for some children to feel grass under their feet and to be able to make a noise without it upsetting anyone.

If there is no such club in your area, ask for them to be considered: they come under different departments in different places, and you may be able to set wheels in motion through a councillor, the social services department or your MP.

First write to the Playleadership Manager at the above address and ask for the GLC Parks Department's excellent coloured illustrated leaflet so that people will be able to see and understand what it is that you are asking them to consider.

One o'clock clubs are urgently needed. I know many of them and well remember one where no less than three mothers came bursting in during the first half an hour saying 'I live for one o'clock!' Many mothers in this area lived in high flats, and they spent the morning doing the housework and saying at intervals: 'Just let's do this . . . and this . . . and now this . . . and soon we shall be going to the one o'clock club, shan't we?' One mother said 'We leave everything tidy, and stay out here until the end, and then go back slowly for tea, and after that it isn't too long until bed so you feel you can cope.'

Drop-in Centres

These are beginning to appear in towns now, some opened by the social services, others run by voluntary bodies. They are intended for anyone who just wants to drop in for a sit, a chat and a cup of tea or coffee. Young mothers and their under-fives are particularly glad to have somewhere definite to go, or they will drop in after shopping. Older people are also happy to be with other people, especially children, for many of them live far away from their grandchildren, and young mothers are often glad to chat with grandparents whose perspective is comfortable with age and experience.

There are toys, books and play activities for the children, and comfortable chairs and books and magazines for the older ones, and a kitchen where sometimes drinks are made and served, but at other times people go and make their own and chat while the kettle boils.

The National Childminding Association
236a High Street, Bromley, Kent BR1 1PQ.

Those parents who are forced to work for long hours each day will need to choose between local authority or private day nurseries, or a childminder. Only you can make this choice, but if choice is available do visit both types of care before deciding: you must have peace of mind, and your child must be happy.

If you choose a day nursery look for peace and quiet as well as plentiful and well used equipment, and a happy relaxed atmosphere where children and staff alike talk and smile quite naturally. Ask how many adults will be sharing the job of mother-substitute.

If you decide that you want your child to be brought up in an ordinary home, by someone who will be a day-time mother in your absence, then go to your local social services department and ask for a list of registered and approved childminders who have vacancies, and visit as many of them as you can. Don't be shy or embarrassed about this: your child is your responsibility and is much too precious to be hastily placed. Remember that although all the childminders and their homes on the list will have been visited and approved they will all be different, and some will be more in tune with you and your particular child than others.

Ask about the daily routine, and the sort of meals that are provided, and whether or not the children are ever smacked. (Childminders are wonderfully honest about this and either say 'I never smack' or 'I treat all the children as I do my own, and if very occasionally I think a smack is called for, then I do'. Only you know which answer is right for you, but ask the question.) Ask what the children do all day (they need water, sand, mud-pies, painting, outdoor play and being read to, as well as play with toys and 'helping' with cooking under the same careful supervision that you would give at home).

As you listen to the answers try to imagine that you are your toddler, about to be left alone here all day and nearly every day, with no means of contacting you, and perhaps not even enough language to tell you in the evening what it has been like all day. Would you feel safe, loved, protected, free to play, not afraid to be 'difficult' on bad days but aware you couldn't 'play up' whenever you liked? And for your part, do you trust her instinctively, find her easy to talk to, not too rigid nor yet too casual?

Don't feel that it is impertinent to ask all these questions and to take up so much time, and don't be afraid of being a nuisance, for every childminder I have ever met says what a relief it is when parents spare the time and care enough to be very particular about where, and with whom, they leave their child.

Mother and Toddler Clubs

There is no national body, but you can contact the Preschool Playgroups Association, Alford House, Aveline Street, London SE11 5DH for information.

A few mother and toddler clubs existed fifty years ago, but in the last ten years there has been a veritable explosion of them up and down the country, testifying to the need mothers have to be together with their children.

There is no uniformity of pattern for each group tries to meet the needs of its own community, but certain common factors begin to emerge. Most of them run for two hours, and in every case the mother or a mother-substitute has to be there throughout the entire time in order to be responsible for her own child, which may be a baby or an under-three (but many mothers have to take older children as well).

There are bricks, paints, push-and-pull toys, dolls, books, dough, slides and toys for the children and chairs for the mothers. The children usually have orange juice and the mothers tea or coffee, for which there is a charge of a few pence. Beyond this the pattern varies. Sometimes one or two volunteers play with the children, or at least prevent them from interfering too badly in each other's play (it is a question of balancing helpfulness and interference), and sometimes another volunteer will make the tea and act as hostess, making sure that no new mother comes in without being welcomed and introduced – and making doubly sure that if one child hurts another both mothers are caught and reassured before they grab their offspring and dash home scarlet-faced and near to tears vowing that they will never return.

There are other groups where the mothers run their own show, taking it in turns to prepare the room, make the tea, collect the tea money, organise fund-raising events for more equipment, and look after the children while the other mothers chat comfortably together with half an eye on their child.

Sometimes the mothers decide they want a speaker up at their end of the room while the children play at the other, and I have met groups who spoke enthusiastically about home-perming sessions, beauty demonstrations, make-do-and-mend classes, first-aid talks and the ever popular 'any problems' discussions with someone from the child guidance clinic.

Sometimes the mothers just enjoy sitting and watching

their children play, marvelling at their length of concentration compared with their play at home. I think space has a lot to do with this. At first children in a large room seldom move further than the distance of 'mother's apron strings', and even later when they are confident they don't always need to roam far as long as they have the feeling that they could if they wanted to – it is when they are cooped up that they become restless. How human!

Other mothers delight in playing with their own children and also other people's children, and once they have gravitated to the children they are usually with them more often than not (this is usually a sign that the mother's own needs have been met). Others just don't want to know about their child at first – their own needs are so pressing. Often it is the mother of whom people say 'She doesn't care, she'd just like to dump and run' who turns out to be a mother who started by caring desperately but found she couldn't cope, and then lost heart and felt a failure, so then something inside her switched off as though she had said to herself: 'You can't go on being hurt and disappointed, guilty and angry like this all the time, and you can't try any harder than you have already tried, or be more anxious and concerned – so forget it, turn your back on the problem, you've already failed as a mother.'

Many of these mothers respond wonderfully to the warmth and friendliness of the group (if the group understands and doesn't freeze them out), and they begin to find that others have had their problems and have found different ways of coping with them that they had not thought of before. They begin to watch their child with other children, and to notice how other mothers cope with wet pants, tumbles, toy snatching, shouting, whining and all the other things that normal children do. They take heart again, switch on again, and respond to their children, who in turn respond to them.

There are mothers on the point of returning to work

who have suddenly learned to enjoy their child with growing confidence and have had the insight to see that the real reason that made them contemplate going back to work so soon wasn't the need for money so much as the need to walk out of an intolerable situation of pain and failure. And they have stayed at home with renewed hope.

One of the steps towards gaining such insights is to be able to talk honestly about the gap between expectations and reality and these three mothers express the feelings of many:

'When I was pregnant I felt sure I'd be lovely, like the mums on the telly adverts, and my toddler would look nice and the home would be shining – not like some of my friends' homes. I've learned since! It's so exhausting, the talking, talking, and sometimes it's so hard to understand. And when she screams and screams, well, I sometimes scream back – I know I'm not supposed to. No, it's definitely *not* like the telly. But I wouldn't be without them – and I'll say this, I think instinct comes into bringing up children.'

'I thought I would be sensible in that I wouldn't be affected by what "they" say, and I wouldn't be caught up in "comparing". But I *am* affected and I'm sure I act badly because of it – because of "comparing". I never thought I would scream and shout, and I feel so awful afterwards.'

'It's the feeling of guilt. There were so many things that I used to resent my mother saying, and I hear myself saying and doing similar things – and it sometimes truly worries me.'

Many mother and toddler groups are realising just how valuable grannies and granny-figures are in giving mothers the trust and confidence to speak freely in this way and to be comforted.

Mother and toddler groups offer a different kind of outlet for other mothers. One said:

'I had a good baby and didn't get depressed, just very bored [until] one day at the shops, another mother stopped and asked me if I would be interested in joining a mother and baby group which was going to open soon. I was really pleased although a bit apprehensive, and she put my name down. From then my life really changed. I had something to get dressed up for at last.

'I had my second child when the first was attending the mother and baby club and I think seeing all the babies helped her in understanding what having a small person in the house would mean. This new baby has been with other children almost from birth and finds it really easy to mix.

'After two years at the club I went on the committee, and now find I can get out in the evenings and talk to other mums. I think if I had not been able to join the club my life would be very dull and I would be a different person. I was always quite shy and at last I feel able to talk to new people and can understand how they feel when they first join the club.'

Other mothers need a model on which to base their growing understanding:

'I think people learn most from watching and listening, learning by example as we're told the children do. Some may not say much at a toddler session, but something goes in and at home again when a situation arises you perhaps recall the better way of dealing with it. I know in my own case I was quick to shout at my two small children, through sheer exhaustion really, but seeing other mums, and the club leader in particular, avoiding a flare-up you realise there are other ways of coping with it, and your children are better off in the long run. You also come to realise that making a noise and a mess are all part of childhood.

'You learn endless ways to amuse and entertain your child in the simplest inexpensive ways, like dough and finger rhymes, water and painting. You try these out at home and suddenly find you're not such a harassed mum after all!'

If you feel like starting a mother and toddler club remember that if it is started 'by' someone 'for' mothers it often ends up with one or two exhausted people waiting on a group of passive mothers. The essence of the venture is that it should be 'our' club with everyone feeling responsible for befriending new mothers and sharing in the work and the fund raising *to boost their own confidence and happiness*, not 'just to get the work done'.

The Pre-school Playgroups Association (PPA)
Alford House, Aveline Street, London SE11 5DH.

Playgroups are intended primarily for three- and four-year-olds, but occasionally there is a small and particularly young group, or a very small one, where a rising-three-year-old is accepted. Playgroups vary in their management even more than mother and toddler groups, and it is particularly important to visit several until you find one that is truly a parent cooperative group, for then there will be a new focus and interest for you as well as your child.

Briefly, a cooperative playgroup is one where about twenty or twenty-four families come together to plan and provide play sessions for their children two or three times a week, or occasionally more. In this they are supported by the Social Services adviser, PPA voluntary workers, and usually by a variety of local meetings and courses that interested people can attend. They share the cost of hiring a hall, and providing materials and equipment.

The play sessions are from two to three hours, and usually one constant playleader and regular helper are engaged to be in the playroom every session, for a token 'thank you' of about £2 and £1·50 each morning. The parents take it in turns, usually two at a time, to be in the playroom each session as well in order that (a) the children shall have plenty of adults to talk and listen with them, read, be available to help when needed, and alert to watch them with enjoyment; (b) so that every parent can have approximately nine or ten free mornings at home for every morning they spend in the playroom; (c) so that parents have the enlightenment of seeing their child with other children, and the fascination of watching them play without the counter-claim of housework; and (d) so that parents can find a new interest to give them incentive to use all their talents, and to discover ones that they didn't know they possessed.

There is a lively community life springing from such playgroups with social evenings, outings, a babysitting service and meetings for discussion and hearing speakers on topics of their choice. Perhaps most valuable of all, many such playgroups have a 'doorstep course' which gives parents the chance to do all the things the children do – paint, clay, dough, cutting and sticking, puzzles and games. As they play they remember their own childhood and how it felt to touch, make, break; to be scolded and praised and called for a meal without warning; to dress up and pretend, make mud-pies and 'play' the piano; to be blamed for something that was a pure accident, and comforted when they were expecting anger.

Parents can identify both with their own childhood feelings and those of their children. 'I'd forgotten . . . I can remember now . . . it all comes back to me,' they say, and in those flashes they see their children anew and extend their understanding of what it is to be a parent.

We are not 'born' good parents (though we have a head

236

start if we had wise and loving parents), and nobody can 'teach' us to be good parents because the relationship between each parent and child, and each mother and father, is unique; there isn't such a thing as 'the right way' to bring up children because if there was it would lead to uniformity of family life which would be intolerable. What there is, overwhelmingly, is the desire of mothers and fathers to learn more about bringing up their own children, in their own family and community, in their own steadily improving way. This learning can best come about in the company of other parents who want to do the same, together with available 'experts' who can fill in some of the gaps in knowledge and understanding.

Obviously I am biased after working in the playgroup movement for fifteen years, but I believe that the birth of this movement heralded something of a revolution in education, for those of us who were once the 'experts' were forced to realise the limits of our expertise, not only by those who didn't want to be 'told' what to do but even more by those who did. What right or justification had we for telling them what was 'best' for their children when we knew so little about the individual parents and circumstances?

Research and experience reveals more and more about children, but only parents can explain where this knowledge fits in with their own present beliefs, attitudes and abilities. Children need a partnership between parents and experts in which child-awareness, self-awareness, and each-other-awareness are balanced so that all of them can grow towards Carlyle's vision:

> Let each become all that
> He was created able of being.
> Expand, if possible, to his full growth
> And show himself at length
> In his own shape and stature
> Be these what they may.

Let the last words rest with the mother of a fifteen-month-old toddler who is learning through love and experience to balance Katie's needs with her own and those of her husband in such a way that, together with Granny's visits, the three generations enhance each other as they adapt to live fully through this present stage of their lives – which is the prelude to the next stage. She wrote:

'Having a toddler is a wonderful, frustrating, exciting, doubtful, joyful, boring, rewarding experience. Its all of these things at different times – although I think the plusses usually outweigh the minuses.

'The way I've managed to cope is to establish a set of priorities – and trying in the main to stick to them.

First – giving your child as much attention as it needs.

Second – giving yourself consideration.

Third – housework subdivided into very definite priority groups

 (a) preparing food
 (b) washing (and ironing as little as possible)
 (c) keeping the house tidy
 (d) cleaning the house.

'My first priority: to me Katie comes first and if she needs feeding, changing or playing with then anything else can wait. This is of course only a general rule, as a spoilt child could result from her always having what she wants at once, and often circumstances dictate that she fits in to our routine – but possibly because I could comply with her wishes she is almost always happy to comply with mine. And for example if I'm peeling the potatoes and Katie brings me a book to read, if they can be left until later I stop and go and read to her. She's usually happy after a few minutes of attention to play on her own again. If, however, my husband is due in in half an hour and the potatoes must be done then she just has to wait (I do try to divert her attention – perhaps by giving her a stool so she can climb up and see what I'm doing).

'My second priority is myself. I find I function best if I have a rest every two hours for half an hour. As this isn't always possible I fit in with Kate's rests. She usually (fortunately for me) sleeps twice in the day for about an hour and a half each time. So I either sit down with my feet up with a good book (science fiction if I can get it) or go back to bed and have a sleep. Don't be surprised if you call on me at 11.00 a.m. and I'm still in my dressing gown. I find if I don't get these 'rest' times I get ratty and irritable with Kate and my husband so I don't feel guilty about taking them – I also found one week when I decided I didn't need to sleep any more in the daytime that I became physically run down and had to see the doctor.

'I also find visiting very therapeutic – old people, sick people, mums with new babies and all my friends. Fortunately I have a car and Katie loves going with me.

'Third is housework. Fortunately I have a very understanding husband who provided there is a meal waiting for him when he comes in at night and he has a clean shirt and hankie every day doesn't worry about the state the house gets into. And it does some days and I don't worry about it. I'll clean it on a good day (or when I have a coffee morning coming up!) or when my mum comes to stay (she's super – she either does the cleaning for me or looks after Kate while I do it).

'I have no desire to go back to "work" yet. How could I possibly miss out on the tears and laughter and sheer enjoyment of the living and learning of my little girl. I don't now regret having her (although there have been times when I wondered why I'd ever wanted to become a mother). But for the occasions like last Sunday in church when she pointed to me and said "Mumma" for the first time (it's usually Daddy) I would never want to be without her.'

All toddlers are not like Katie, and all parents are not like Katie's parents, but I commend to you the idea of working out your own priorities in such a way that all of you have your *basic essentials* met each day. If you think of it as 'give us this day our daily bread', you can better accept that the butter and jam can come later as your child becomes more independent and dependable, and you will be correspondingly free to find new avenues for personal growth that enrich you and your family yet again.

The National Housewives Register (NHR)
National Organiser, Gants Mill, Bruton, Somerset BA10 0DB.

Not all mothers are maternal, and indeed those who are don't always want to think and talk only about children and domesticity. If you are one of these then joining a local group of like-minded people, meeting in one another's homes, to talk about matters both serious and lighthearted may be just the refresher you need. Write to the National Organiser and she will send you the name of your nearest local organiser, who will put you in touch with your nearest group.

Recipes for Play Dough

Tip a small bag (500 g) of *self-raising flour* into a bowl. Make a well in the centre, add a little water from a 1 pint measure and with your hands or a fork mix it in lightly. Add a little more water and continue to mix lightly until the damp pieces begin to hold together and place on one side. Make another well, add more water, and continue the process until all the flour is incorporated in the dough balls (the amount of water you need varies slightly according to the grade of flour; you may need slightly more or less). Put all the balls back in the bowl together and work with your hands until you have a smooth soft lump, neither wet enough to feel sticky nor so dry that pieces crumble away.

When this dough is made you will find that it is rather like a lump of elastic, it can be stretched and twisted, even swung like a rope. You can nip, squeeze, pummel and punch, and as you take your hands away the holes and dents fill up again.

Your child may enjoy the lump plonked down on a smooth table top just as it is, but he may also like to sit comfortably and have it in his lap. Dough is very clean and a cotton apron or one of dad's old shirts worn back to front is protection enough.

A large wooden spoon is sometimes a helpful accompaniment, and if you try smacking the dough as hard as you can you will see why! The sound and the 'feel' are most satisfying, and the dough will absorb pent-up energy of body and emotion.

If your toddler should say with great satisfaction 'I'm smacking the baby!' don't be alarmed. This is nature's way of releasing deep feelings through play where no harm will be done. Accept that he resents the baby sometimes and don't make him feel guilty about it, or about smacking his substitute baby; just be glad that he has found a safe outlet and say something like 'That makes a lovely sound, doesn't it?' or 'Does that feel very good?' You will innocently be referring to the dough and the spoon, but the unspoken communication between you is that you understand each other without the need for any direct reference to the real baby at all. When his spoon-wielding arm is tired he will probably turn the spoon round and poke holes with the handle instead. Or you can offer butter beans, large buttons or other objects to be hidden up in the dough. He can push them in, but the dough will push them out again, so he will have to bury them deeper and the play will change its nature yet again.

At the end of the play wrap the dough in a plastic bag and put it in the fridge or somewhere cool and it will last for about a week before it begins to smell sour. You may need to dust it with more flour if it becomes sticky during play, or to wet your hands and work more water in if the heat of the room and warm hands begin to dry it out too much.

This dough will not keep as long as one that contains a large handful of salt and this just has to be accepted: the two recipes make quite different types of dough and you will only get the yielding elastic quality by omitting salt.

You can try wholemeal flour, or add oatmeal for a different feel as a change. And in a year or so, when fingers, hands and wrists are bigger and stronger, you can try *strong flour* – the elastic quality is so strong that it takes a real effort to manipulate it at all.

Salt-free dough is kindest to sore or very dry hands, and a tablespoonful of oil will make it still more soothing.

Books

The following books have all been written by people who understand and care about parents as well as children. They are equally on the side of both because they see so clearly that children and parents interact with each other and can either add to each other's happiness and well-being, or frustrate each other.

They all convey the importance of play but make it clear that real play can't be 'used' as a means of 'getting children on', neither is it just 'go and play with your toys'. Play is nature's way of preparing children naturally for all the learning that will follow in later years; and the parents' attitude to their children, themselves, and childhood as a state in its own right, is all-important.

The Vital Years and Your Child, Audrey Bilski (Souvenir)

Pre-school Activities, Dorothy and John Pickering (Batsford)

Playing, Learning and Living, Vera Roberts (Black)

Pre-school Play, Kenneth Jameson and Pat Kidd (Studio Vista)

*Supertot, Jean Marzollo, illustrated by Irene Trivas (Allen & Unwin)

*Mother's Help, edited by Susan Dickinson, illustrated by Shirley Hughes (Collins)

*Playgroup Activities (just as suitable for home), PPA, Alford House, Aveline Street, London SE11 5DH

*Growing Up With Good Food, The National Childbirth Trust (Leeds Branch), 9 Queensborough Terrace, Bayswater, London W2 3TB; new edition to be published by Unwin Paperbacks in 1982.

*What's A House? (see section on Scribble and Daub), Kenneth Jameson and Brenda Crowe, by post from Galt Toys Ltd (see catalogue address)

Accident Prevention and First Aid in Playgroups (just as suitable for the home) PPA, Alford House, Aveline Street, London

Help! (First Aid for everyday emergencies) (Collins)

**The Good Toy Guide*, The Toy Libraries Association, Seabrook House, Wyllyotts Manor, Darkes Lane, Potters Bar, Herts, EN6 2HL

*These books are specially recommended for those who don't have much time or inclination for reading, and who like the essential wisdom and practicalities to come through clearly, lightly and accurately, which doesn't mean that they are any the less valuable for avid readers.

The following books are comprehensive guides from birth onwards: they are long, but so clearly laid out and indexed that you can find just what you want without feeling you have to sit down and read from beginning to end!

Baby and Child Care, Dr Benjamin Spock (W. H. Allen)
Book of Child Care, Dr Hugh Jolly (Allen & Unwin)
Baby and Child, Penelope Leach (Michael Joseph)

Inoculations and Quarantine

Some parents are having second thoughts about inoculations against whooping cough, so discuss this carefully between yourselves and with your doctor. But do discuss tetanus (lockjaw) and polio as separate issues, for these can kill or cripple for life.

If you or your children catch German measles be sure to let people know before visiting them or inviting them home lest someone is in the early stages of pregnancy, for German measles early in pregnancy can seriously affect the unborn baby. If you become pregnant, and then discover that you have been in contact, report it to your doctor at once.

Catalogues

The following catalogues are well worth sending for and studying together for they complement each other and will help you to balance your budget and your children's play needs.

James Galt Toys Limited Brookfield Road, Cheadle, Cheshire, SK8 2PF

Paul & Marjorie Abbatt Toys Limited Esavian Works, Fairview Road, Stevenage, Herts SG1 2NX

Both the above firms stock a comprehensive range of top-quality classic children's toys, painting equipment, climbing apparatus, bookcases and a wide assortment of storage units. All the items are available by post.

Community Playthings Darvell, Robertsbridge, East Sussex TN32 5DR

Every piece that is made by the craftsmen woodworkers of this Society of Brothers is a thing of beauty, precision and strength. The prices are high, largely because the toys and apparatus are intended for group play use, but a child would be privileged to possess one of these items for its aesthetic as well as its play value; we deprive children quite seriously if they never handle natural materials and craftsmanship.

Fisher-Price Toys Limited PO Box 47, Northampton NN1 2QG

The characteristic toys of this firm are brightly coloured with a strong fantasy element. Plastic, painted wood, and often built-in sound effects combine together to give safe and durable toys.

Mothercare-by-Post Post Office Box 145, Cherry Tree
    Road, Watford, Herts WD2 5SH
This firm stocks a good range of aids to safety for the
kitchen, bathroom and stairs, and some very tough and
well designed polythene and polypropylene push, pull and
riding toys.

What Every Mum Should Know British Standards
    Institution, Consumer Affairs Department, 2 Park
    Street, London W1A 2BS
Every family should send for this booklet which explains
that 'Some products e.g. carrycot stands, fireguards and
toys have to satisfy Government Regulations which are
based on standards, so you can be pretty certain that these
goods will be safe.' Over and above this safeguard some
products carry the Kitemark and a number, e.g. BS3254
or BS AU 157a on car safety seats. This booklet gives the
Kitemark number to look for on dummies, wooden- and
metal-framed cots, cot mattresses and pillows, fireguards,
car safety seats, webbing harness for prams, pushchairs,
and high chairs, carrycots and stands, medicine cabinets,
safety barriers, walking frames, rigid-sided playpens, and
toys.

It is worth knowing that 95 per cent of British toy
manufacturers belong to the British Toy Manufacturers'
Association and they make sure their members' products
are made to BS3443. There are also Government Regulations which make it illegal to sell dangerous toys.

The Royal Society for the Prevention of Accidents, Home
    Safety Dept, Cannon House, The Priory, Queensway,
    Birmingham B4 6BS
Road Safety and Home Safety information is always
worth having, especially from such a reputable source.